Educational Dimensions of School Buildings

Edited by
Jan Bengtsson

Educational Dimensions of School Buildings

PETER LANG
Frankfurt am Main · Berlin · Bern · Bruxelles · NewYork · Oxford · Wien

Bibliographic Information published by the Deutsche Nationalbibliothek
The Deutsche Nationalbibliothek lists this publication in the Deutsche Nationalbibliografie; detailed bibliographic data is available in the internet at http://dnb.d-nb.de.

The publication of this book was kindly supported
by the Längmanian Foundation for Culture
and by the Wilhelm and Martina Lundgren´s
Research Foundation.

Cover illustration:
Rebecka Nordström Graf

ISBN 978-3-631-63046-4
© Peter Lang GmbH
Internationaler Verlag der Wissenschaften
Frankfurt am Main 2011
All rights reserved.

All parts of this publication are protected by copyright. Any utilisation outside the strict limits of the copyright law, without the permission of the publisher, is forbidden and liable to prosecution. This applies in particular to reproductions, translations, microfilming, and storage and processing in electronic retrieval systems.

www.peterlang.de

Table of Contents

Introduction 7

Educational significations in school buildings 11
Jan Bengtsson

The space of the school as a changing educational tool 35
Patrick Bjurström

Architecture, pedagogy and children
The intersection between different action programs in school 49
Thomas Gitz-Johansen, Jan Kampmann and Inge Mette Kirkeby

Interspaces for learning?
A study of corridors in some Swedish schools in a historical perspective 75
Maj-Lis Hörnqvist

The school building as experience 99
Hansjorg Hohr

About the authors 117

Introduction

Jan Bengtsson

One way of defining a modern society is by way of compulsory schooling. Understood in this way, every modern society offers elementary schooling to all its citizens. The purpose of schooling is that all citizens acquire basic skills in reading, writing, mathematics, etc. in order to be able to participate in and influence society. Such a society is in principle a democratic society. Thus, in modern societies almost all adults have passed through the school buildings and spent many years in them.

As a consequence of compulsory schooling, schoolteachers are the largest professional group in modern societies. School buildings are the workplace of all these teachers. It is thus hard to find any kind of building that is more used than school buildings. In spite of this, we know surprisingly little about the influence of these buildings on the work of the teachers and the learning of the pupils – both in the narrow sense of learning the subject matters of the school and in the wider sense of the disciplining effects of the school buildings.

Educational research has a rather strong focus on the cognitive activities of teaching and learning and tends to neglect the material world as well as the human body. It would seem to be an important task to complement the cognitive focus; not with a purely material focus, but with a perspective that includes the relationship between cognitive and material aspects as well as other dimensions of teaching and learning. In this way, it will be possible to offer a more differentiated picture of teaching and learning in schools.

This book is a contribution to the understanding of the relationship between school buildings and those who work in them, teachers as well as pupils. Seven scholars from different countries offer different theoretical perspectives and empirical results to understand school buildings. Both architectonical and educational researchers contribute to the book. I believe that the book might reveal some of the educational dimensions of school buildings. Hence, the choice of title for the book.

In the first chapter, Jan Bengtsson uses a life-world approach to make a phenomenological analysis of educational significations in school buildings and their epistemological consequences for the study of the impact of school buildings on pupils' and teachers' experience and use of school buildings. In a narrow sense, educational significations in school buildings are limited to the building's influence on teachers' teaching activities. In a wider sense, educational significations in school buildings include all the disciplining or socialising dimensions of the buildings, which could be called *the silent education of school buildings.* All parts and objects of the school refer to each other and to the people working there, and together they constitute a particular regional world of educational significations that are revealed in the experience and use by teachers and pupils.

In the second chapter, Patrick Bjurström introduces Bill Hillier's and Julienne Hanson's space syntax theory as an architect's tool to understand school buildings. The discussion is guided by the question in what sense a *school building* can be comprehended *as a tool* for teaching and learning, and, further, how such a tool can be improved. As an architect, Bjurström looks upon the function of the building as an educational tool not only in terms of the equipment of each room or their technical and aesthetic quality. Following the space syntax theory, he sees the practical effect of architecture on human social behaviour at the level of space, particularly the way the parts of space are connected.

In the third chapter, Thomas Gitz-Johansen, Jan Kampmann and Inge Mette Kirkeby take their point of departure in Bruno Latour's actor-network theory. In particular, they make use of his concept of *programme action* to analyse the practice of three different schools in Denmark. The action programme is used to analyse both physical space and persons as actors who interact with and influence each other. The authors explore how school architecture influences the teacher's possibilities and how tension may arise between educational ideas and ideas built into the physical space of the schools. They also discuss not only the way education and architecture may exercise different kinds of social control over the pupils, but also how the school building, seen from the children's perspectives, can be an obstacle to or a resource for the children's own activities and goals.

In the fourth chapter, Maj-Lis Hörnqvist takes a look at the varying usage and function of interspaces in school buildings in the last 100 years. As the view of education changes through the years, so does the educational signification of interspaces. The educational significations of interspaces were studied by observing twenty different schools in different parts of Sweden. As a theoretical frame of reference, Otto Friedrich Bollnow's phenomenological theory of lived space was used, particularly *the space of action, the mood of space* and *the space of human relations.*

In the fifth chapter, Hansjörg Hohr discusses the effect of school buildings on their users from the perspective of Alfred Lorenzer's theory of socialization and experience. Three types of experience are proposed. There is pre-symbolic experience, called *feeling,* which is fundamental and is the first step in socialization constituting the basic psychological structure. Then there is sensuous-symbolic experience, called *aesthetic experience,* which is mediated by aesthetic interaction. The ethos of the school building is articulated on this level. Third, although rather marginal, there is discursive-symbolic experience, called *con-*

ceiving, mediated by propositional speech. On this level, one finds the discursive qualities of the school building. Finally, the functionality of the school building – an aspect of the three types of experience – is discussed on the basis of concepts of knowledge, power and control.

Educational significations in school buildings

Jan Bengtsson

The compulsory elementary school was established in Sweden by a law in 1842. According to this elementary school law, every parish in the country should start up an elementary school within five years and employ an approved teacher. In the following decades, buildings were created for this particular purpose. Schooling in Sweden has thus been located in special school buildings for more than 150 years. This means that all the pupils and teachers are accustomed to these buildings in their everyday life, and every adult has many years of experience of them from his/her own schooldays. With the exception of the small children, everybody seems to know what a school building is. In spite of this, one cannot expect that those who use the school can tell what signification the school buildings have for the people working in them. Probably the opposite is the case. Those who use the school know it inside out and know how it can be used. It is for just this reason that they do not have a distance to the school. They have implicit functional knowledge of how the school works, but not explicit knowledge of the school and what it does with its users. There is a lack of distance between building and user that prevents them from noticing it before it makes itself felt. For this reason, small children may draw our attention to things that we have not noticed before or that we have not seen for long time and have forgotten. An example is the child who asks why the old city school has such big doors. Do the giants' children go to that school? It thus seems as if teachers and pupils are in the power of the school buildings rather than the other way round.

There exists, however, a profession that can be expected to have explicit knowledge of buildings – the architectural profession. Architects draw buildings for all kinds of purposes, including schools. Architects, by virtue of their profession, have a distance to buildings. However, they do not have educational knowledge, and to give the building an educational shape, they need instructions from the commissioner of the building, which has always been the state, the municipality or a private establishment. In Sweden, a working group is usually formed when planning for a new school, and the group usually includes the buyer (property manager), the user (head of the school, teachers and other staff) and the architect. Holm (1999) and Mårtensson (1999) divide the planning into different phases, the most important of which are framing and projection. From an educational point of view, the architectural commission seems to be fairly general in its formulation, limited to information about the school's location at the place, type of school, number of pupils, different types of rooms, etc., whereas economical frameworks and technical specifications can be detailed. In private schools, however, it is possible to find pronounced and sometimes very detailed educational ideas that the architect is supposed to realise in the building. Waldorf schools are examples of schools that express educational ideas in everything, from choice of place, form of rooms and colours to furnishing. In the same way as the curriculum, instructions about the public school building's design have varied in the amount of detail throughout history and no longer exist, at least in Sweden (Bjurström, 2004 a). The less explicit instructions about the design of the building in educational terms, the more the architectonic design of the educational choices will be left to people who certainly know architecture, but who, as far as education is concerned, have to rely on experiences from their own schooldays, on trends circulating at the time and/or ideas presented by the planning group.

If the present knowledge situation about the school building's signification for those who work in school corresponds with the above description, there is an apparent need for explicit knowledge in the case of educational practitioners as well as working school architects. This field of knowledge has been a neglected area in research in the Scandinavian countries and elsewhere. In recent years, however, there has been a growing interest in educational research as well as in architectural research (e.g. Björklid, 2005; Bjuström, 2004 b; Böhme, 2009; Burke & Grosvenor, 2003; Cold, 2002; David & Weinstein, 1987; Dudek, 2000 a, 2000 b; Eriksen, 1996; Gitz-Johansen, Kampmann & Kirkeby, 2001; Jelik & Kemnitz, 2003; de Jong, 1995; Kristenson, 1997, 1998, 1999; Kristenson & Balgård, 1995; *Krut,* 1995, 2003; Lindblad, 1993; Lindholm, 1995; Olsson, 1995; Rosén, 1995; Skantze, 1989, 1995; Stahle, 1999; Törnquist 2005; Ulleberg, 1996). What results this research may bring about and what practical consequences it may have depends, however, on the philosophical point of departure.[1] In philosophy, the ontological and epistemological theories are of primary interest. In this context, I intend to discuss school buildings' ontology and epistemological consequences from a life-world approach.

A life-world approach to the study of school buildings

The life-world approach is based on the phenomenological concept of the life-world and should, therefore, be seen as part of the phenomenological movement. It has, however, its own distinguishing characteristics and this justifies its own name (Bengtsson, 2005). Very briefly, I want to delineate some salient features of the life-world approach and then use it in a discussion of school buildings' ontology and its epistemological consequences. This implies, among other things, that philosophy's general procedure is replaced by philosophical ques-

---

1 A preliminary outline of the knowledge in this field of research can be found in Alerby, Bengtsson, Hörnqvist and Kroksmark, 2002.

tions of a regional kind. In this way, the gap between philosophy and empirical research on school buildings can be bridged.

The life-world was originally a philosophical concept with an ontological as well as an epistemological meaning. This particular view of reality and knowledge can be used for empirical research on educational significations in school buildings and give it its own direction among contemporary research approaches.

One epistemological implication of the life-world theory is that all knowledge production takes the life-world for granted and presupposes it in empirical research as well as in philosophical reflection. The life-world can in this sense be said to be pre-scientific as well as pre-reflective. Based on this epistemology, both researchers who make empirical studies and philosophers who reflect on the conditions of empirical research are intertwined with the world, and their knowledge is conditioned by this worldly relationship. Consequently, empirical research and philosophical reflection cannot claim privileged access to reality that warrants final knowledge.

From an ontological point of view, the life-world represents a pluralistic and integrative view of reality. Expressed in relation to traditional Western ontology, this pluralism means that reality cannot be completely understood with the help of a limited number of kinds of qualities, such as material and mental qualities. Instead, reality is conceived as a complex reality that consists of a large number of different qualities that cannot be reduced to each other.

A second major characteristic of life-world ontology is the intertwining or interdependence between life and world. This is what the integrative view stands for and it rejects dualistic ontology. The life-world is neither an objective world in itself nor a subjective world, but an ambiguous world in between. World and life are mutually dependent on each other. In this way, life and world are an original unity that only afterwards can be separated into different parts. It is, therefore, a mistake to force us to choose between life and world, as we have learnt to do in the history of ontology.

This point of view implies an understanding of reality more in terms of "both and" instead of "either or". This understanding is not only applied to life and world, but also to body and mind, object and subject, outer and inner, physical and mental, sensuous and cognitive, self and other, individual and society, etc. Consequently, particular things, buildings and places can tell us what kind of people live or have been living there. They are significant. A computer, for instance, is not a material thing in itself, but it is also an expression of a particular embodied subject, situated in history and the world, and with corresponding possible actions and experiences, dreams and memories, values and norms, etc.

Because the world is always united with the life of a human being, it is an uncompleted and open world. The life-world might be described as the world of everything that is possible to experience and do. Every life-world could be said to be surrounded by an outer horizon. The horizon of the present world ends, but a horizon is not an absolute border. It can always be displaced. In daily life, the world is delimited to regional worlds, which are oriented around different activities such as work, home life and leisure activities. The regional worlds are parts of the life-world, and consist of things, buildings, persons, etc. related to each other through activities and specific to its regional world.

Individual human beings can also be understood in a corresponding way, since they are united with the world. If something is changed in the world, the individual changes accordingly. For instance, when the computer is replaced by pen and paper or the opposite, when the computer replaces pen and paper, it is not only a change of physical things in an objective world, but the individual changes as well. In a similar way, the identity of a person is not limited to the identity of one particular regional world, but changes between the different regional worlds. An individual human being should thus not be understood as an independent or absolute identity. Consequently, it is of significance in what worlds humans are living and who is living in particular worlds.

Educational significations as a basic concept in the ontology of school buildings

Ontological options in understanding educational significations

I noted above that architects, from more or less detailed instructions, are realising educational ideas in the school buildings. It would, therefore, be possible to say that the architect's intentions are materialised in the building. Such a statement expresses a particular ontological point of view that is not compatible with all ontologies in history and the present day. A dualistic ontology, for instance, may certainly include both ideas and matter, but they cannot be united. The buildings only consist of the physical matter they are built out of, but not of ideas. On the other hand, educational-architectonical ideas may be found in the thoughts of the architect, but they are mental and not material. This implies that buildings and educational-architectonical ideas are separated into two separate and incompatible worlds: one material and one intellectual/mental. I find it difficult, however, to see how school buildings can be separated from other kinds of buildings if only the material qualities are considered. It is first when educational ideas are materialised in a building that the building becomes a school building.

A dualistic view of buildings also limits the ability to acquire knowledge about buildings. By means of an empirical study of school buildings, it is only possible to acquire knowledge about the building's material qualities, and among these qualities there are no educational qualities. If we want knowledge

Educational significations 15

about school education, we must address the architect or the teacher and his/her inner thoughts.

From a life-world ontology, however, one may expect to acquire knowledge about school buildings' educational content by means of empirical studies of the buildings. Houses are both significant and filled with significations. With these two expressions, I want to suggest that there are significations in houses and, for this reason, that they concern us (Herklint, 2000). They may even become a part of peoples' identity, an invisible architecture in the people (Werne, 1987). Houses are never neutral matter. School buildings express educational significations that impact on people working there and they are available for interpretation by empirical researchers.

Educational significations as individual and collective

But how should the educational significations of school buildings be understood? What are the significations that affect people and that can be interpreted? Could they be identified by the intentions that the individual architect puts into the building (e.g. Besset, 1992; Hart, 1993) or should they be understood as general significations that can be found in all school buildings (e.g. Norberg-Schulz, 1980, 1985; Thiis-Evensen, 1987)? From a life-world perspective neither of these alternatives seems to be exhaustive. Every distinguished architect certainly expresses his or her own intentions in the buildings that they build, but the buildings produced during a certain period of time soon display characteristics typical of the period. This is an expression of the worldliness and the historicity of the intentions. School buildings present both a collective style and individual solutions.

A survey of Swedish secondary schools from around 1900 to 2000 reveals big differences typical of the period. The period around 1900 presents schools in a national romantic style. Many buildings are big and dark with inspiration from palaces, castles and monasteries, and they are surrounded by schoolyards with walls or high railings. Nordhemsskolan in Gothenburg is a powerful expression of this style (figure 1).

Figure 1: Nordhemsskolan, Gothenburg, built in 1914–1917. Architects: Arvid Bjerke and R. O. Swensson.

In the 1920s, functionalism started to manifest itself, and the castles were replaced by pared down and light buildings with the motto "less is more" (Mies van der Rohe). Gunnar Asplund was a prominent figure in this movement in Sweden and he was also the architect of a school in Gothenburg (Olson, 1992) (figure 2). There remain, however, neoclassical elements in this school, but it was also designed as early as in 1917. The representatives of Swedish functionalism introduced functionalism as "a new objectivity" (Asplund, Gahn, Markelius, Paulsson, Sundahl, Åhrén, 1931) with efficiency and rationality as guiding stars, and with its balanced proportions it was aesthetically pleasing (figure 3). Viewing the school as a place for educational engineering fits well into the functionalistic ideology.

Educational significations 17

Figure 2: Karl Johansskolan, Gothenburg, built in 1922–1925. Architect: Gunnar Asplund.

Figure 3: Eriksdalsskolan, Stockholm, built in 1937–1938. Architects: Nils Ahrbom and Helge Zimdahl.

In the post-war period during the 1950s, with its belief in the future, functionalism was very influential in Sweden, but it moved out of the city centres to the new suburbs, where it found new ways of expression in surroundings consisting of smaller blocks of flats with room for natural environment. Norra Örnässkolan in Luleå (figure 4) and Sturebyskolan in Stockholm are good examples of schools in such an environment.

Figure 4: Norra Örnässkolan, Luleå, built in 1952. Architect: John Berglund.

In the left-leaning 1970s, the schools moved to new large-scale housing areas and were linked to shopping centres to be a part of the rest of the society. Consequently, the exterior of the school buildings are often invisible and the interior of the school buildings with study halls resemble open factory halls where the work is done collectively. The daylight in the schoolrooms often comes from skylights and light wells. Henry Pluckrose gave this view of school a theoretical formulation in his book *Open School, Open Society* (1975). This school type is well represented in Sweden and can be exemplified by many individual school buildings, such as Björkskataskolan in Luleå (figure 5), Öxnehagaskolan in Jönköping, Ärvingeskolan in Stockholm, and Skälltorpskolan in Gothenburg.

Educational significations 19

Figure 5: Björkskataskolan, Luleå, built in 1976. Architect: Dan Lundbäck.

At the turn of the millennium, new schools were built in new housing areas with terraced houses and detached houses. The school buildings are once again detached, but because of a post-modernistic organisation of the school buildings in a frequently kaleidoscopic distribution of house-elements in different planes, with glazed surfaces, different heights, colours, materials, etc. it may still be difficult to determine the identity of the building. The inner rooms have become more human in their proportions with straight corridors, rectangular classrooms and open study halls being replaced by delimited working units with space for work in classes as well as in smaller groups, but also the inner room of the school has thus become less visible. Kråkbergsskolan in Sunderbyn just outside Luleå is a good example of a post-modernistic school building (figure 6).

Figure 6: Kråkbergsskolan, Luleå, built in 1992, Architect: Mats Jakobsson.

The similarities typical of the period that are found in school architecture in no way exclude individual differences in one and the same period. Gunnar Asplund's architecture is certainly typical of the period, but it definitely stands out from the rest.

The different periods of school buildings that can be identified during the last century show that the history of school buildings cannot be understood as a simple continuity and development, but existing materialized educational intentions are replaced by new materialized intentions. The practical consequence of this situation is that the use of older school buildings contains tensions and conflicts between user and building. Tensions and conflicts between user and building may also occur when old teachers are moved to new school buildings.

The educational significations that are materialised in buildings are thus individually collective. This implies that they are relative to historical and individual circumstances. Consequently, the significations cannot be understood as general in a universal sense. Certain forms do recur through history, but to avoid being completely insipid and dull they have to be filled with a concrete content, and this is always done in mundane relative circumstances. It is first in its materialised form that the education of architecture has a signification for us, but at the same time older school buildings' educational significations are foreign and require an effort to be understood. The same also applies, of course, to the school buildings of other cultures.

Intentions of educational signification and unintentional consequences

The significations that the architect designs into the school buildings may be intentional, but do not always have to be. In principle, one could say that the fewer educational instructions that are included in the architect's commission and the less educational knowledge the architect has, the fewer educational ideas are intentionally designed into the building. This does not mean, however, that the buildings lose or lack educational significations. All buildings are filled with significations, either intentionally or not, and school buildings are filled with educational significations, even if the architect did not have a single educational intention as regards the building. One example is the palace-like schools that were built at the beginning of the 20th century in many countries. With their large-scale measurements and austere lines, their heaviness and elevation, these schools could make the children feel small, negligible, vulnerable and subordinated. In the spirit of Foucault (e.g. 1974), one might say that the school disciplines the children to take on a subservient attitude already at the large and heavy irongate (figure 7). This signification is confirmed by the huge building that loom large in front of them (figure 8), by the large open schoolyard that they have to cross in order to reach the imposing entrance doors (figure 9), the large staircase with the large steps (figure 10) and by the choice of material and the idiom of the school.

Figure 7: Nordhemsskolan, Gothenburg, built in 1914–1917. Architects: Arvid Bjerke and R. O. Swensson.

Educational significations 23

Figure 8: Torpaskolan, Jönköping, built in 1907–1908. Architect: August Atterström.

Figure 9: Torpaskolan, Jönköping, built in 1907–1908, architect August Atterström.

Educational significations 25

Figure 10: Mariaskolan, Stockholm, built 1893. Architect: Ernst Haegglund.

The question is, however, whether the disciplining signification was the intention of this architecture. The architect could have had the intention, by the same means of expression, to lend status to the school and give it a distinct symbolic value in society. But this symbol language is addressed to adults, and one unintentional consequence is the significations that the building has for the children. Another example, closer to Foucault's example from the disciplining effect of prisons built according to the principle of a panopticon (1974), is the post-modernistic schools from the end of the 20th century and beginning of the 21st century. These buildings, with their glass walls and transparency, discipline many children to work on their assignments even if they are alone in the room, because they know that they might be seen at any time, even if no teacher is present in the room. This architecture might also give an unpleasant feeling of always being observed and controlled. The intention of the architect could, however, have been limited to creating open and light rooms and making visible the different activities going on in the building. But once again, this does not exclude the educational signification that the architecture may have for the children. Irrespective of what the intentions of the architect might have been, which can be difficult or impossible to find out, the building always has certain educational significations that have an effect on people.

Educational significations are dependent on the building's material, but not identical with it

Using the life-world perspective, school buildings could be said to contain a materialised educational programme in the sense that educational significations not only have a particular content and are mundanely relative, but are also dependent on the building's material. The significations are in the physical building: in the gravel in the schoolyard, in the heavy oak door, in the granite stairs and the forged banisters, in the clothes-pegs, in the wooden desks, in the deep window-recesses, in the whiteboard, in the corridors, in the classrooms, in the glass walls, etc. But the educational signification cannot be identified with the material. An analysis of the material does not help us understand the educational significations. The educational signification of stairs, for instance, will never emerge from an analysis of the material, irrespective of how exhaustive it may be. It is something different and more than, for instance, granite, and its signification appears in embodied and lived experience and understanding.

The school building's liberation from the architect

The intentions that the architect once has had are thus materialised in the school buildings. This implies that they have been liberated from the architect and become available for everybody to understand and interpret. The educational signification is in the building and not in the architect, and it is only in this way that it can signify something for people. If the significations only existed in the architect's intentions, school buildings would not be able to signify anything for us. And if the signification were only available through an understanding of the architect's intentions, the school buildings would cease to signify something when there is no longer access to the intentions. Consequently, the architect cannot claim any priority of interpretation when it comes to significations of buildings. In the same way as the architect leaves the building when the project is finished, one might say that the building leaves the architect and starts its own life. In the independent life of the school building, when it has begun to be used by its users, the architect, as time passes, becomes anonymous and is not noticed anymore.

Educational significations in a narrow and a wide sense

In a narrow sense, only specific objects and rooms in school buildings are understood as being educational. This usually applies to objects such as pointers, rulers, whiteboards, desks and books as well as rooms such as classrooms, gymnasiums, handicraft room, music room and other specialised rooms. In a wider sense, educational significations are not limited to specific objects and rooms, but include schoolyards, stairs, doors, corridors, toilets, refectories, lighting, clocks, etc. Furthermore, educational signification varies with the organisation of the desks in the classroom, the use of the corridors, the location of the classroom and other rooms, the room for separate group work, the kinds of room that exist, the technical equipment they have, the delimitation of the schoolyard from surrounding buildings, etc. This implies that school buildings as a whole, both their external and internal architecture, as well as the schoolyard and the school's location in society, have educational signification. Also the school's size, in terms of the number of children that have to share a limited area, has educational signification.

All the different parts of the school refer to each other and to the people who work there, and together they constitute a specific regional world of educational significations that give meaning to the different parts. This world is a practical and social world. Consequently, school buildings can be said to offer possible forms of educational practice or to offer a certain organisation of educational activity. It is, however, necessary to distinguish between the school as a practice for the teachers' teaching and the school as a practice for the pupils' learning. The former practice is a professional practice, and working in this kind of practice is a liberal choice, whereas the latter practice is compulsory for all Swedish children between 7 and 16 years of age. The children have to go to school every day irrespective whether they have difficulties with schoolwork or whether they like it or not. It is thus necessary to differentiate between the function of school buildings for the teachers and for the pupils and how well or badly they support each other.

But it is also necessary to bear in mind that the school buildings not only influence teaching and learning through their significations, they also educate or discipline their users in a wider sense. This kind of influence could be called "silent education" in contrast to the expressed education that can be found in the curriculum, the schoolbooks and the teaching. Silent education should also be distinguished from the hidden curriculum that is the unintended education of schoolteachers' activities (Jackson, 1968). Silent education is education by the educational significations of the building and its equipment.

The scope of educational significations

What, then, is the scope of school buildings' educational significations? There are undoubtedly large differences between possible and actual educational significations in a school building. The educational ideas that were materialised in schools around 1900 were in many respects very different from the ideas that guide the building of schools in 2000. Most of these schools are still in use. This does not imply, however, that the activity in these schools has to be as old as the schools. The schools may to some extent have been rebuilt and the furniture may have been rearranged or changed with the intention of adding new educational significations to the school buildings. Significations also change meaning in the eyes and hands of new teachers. One interesting example is a school from the 1970s in Stockholm (Ärvingeskolan) that had lost its schoolyard. According to the drawings of the school, there was a large and park-looking schoolyard that was shared with the adjacent housing area and shopping centre. Addicts had, however, started to use the place as a meeting-place. As a result, the teachers did not think that there was a schoolyard.

No matter how much is changed in old school buildings, there always remain significations that become so natural that they to a certain degree control the educational activities. Buildings can never be without signification for us. The degree of influence depends on what the teachers and pupils are able to do with the buildings. In new school buildings, the opposite situation may prevail, that is, that certain significations are not used or observed. This is often the case with new technology, new planning and other innovations that are foreign to the teachers who are first to work in the new school. In practice, this means that the significations do not exist.

Epistemological consequences

Against this background it is not evident that we can acquire knowledge about school buildings' educational significations by asking the architect who designed the school. The intentions of the architect can for several reasons not be identified by the educational significations of the building. Firstly, school buildings have educational significations without our knowledge of the architect's intentions. Secondly, school buildings have educational significations regardless of whether they were intended by the architect or not. Thirdly, educational significations in "the same building" change over time and in the eyes and hands of different users. The knowledge that we can acquire of school buildings' educational significations by asking the architect thus seems to be limited, but it may provide a valuable perspective and addition to the understanding of a specific school building.

It does not seem to be easier, however, to obtain knowledge of a school's educational significations by asking teachers and pupils about them. They are certainly at school almost every day and experience them everywhere. Teachers and pupils have extensive practical and functional knowledge that has settled in their lived bodies and gives them confidence and a sense of security when they act in the school buildings (Bengtsson, 1993). This knowledge, however, is not explicit cognitive knowledge of the educational significations in practice and it does not need to be connected with words, although human beings can be said to be linguistic by virtue of their existence. Linguisticity only means that human beings are able to use language, not that they have a language for everything that they experience. For people who live in a recurring practice day after day, this practice is easily taken for granted, as the natural and the right way of acting and understanding. The practical consequence of this immersion in daily activities is that the practitioners lack the necessary distance to be able to talk about them. It is well known that the closest often is the most strange to us.

However, we are not dependent on the teachers' and pupils' ability to talk about educational significations in order to obtain knowledge about them. The educational significations are not in the teachers and the pupils, but in the material building, although not identical with its material. The pupils and the teachers reveal the educational significations in their experience and use of the building. Experience of the school, however, is not of a predicative, cognitive or reflective kind, but rather pre-predicative, pre-cognitive or pre-reflective, that is, lived and embodied experience. The educational significations appear in the encounter between the lived body and the material building. The organization of tables and materials in the classroom as well as the kind of tables and chairs may facilitate or obstruct cooperation between the pupils simply by making it easy or difficult to move around. The choice of furniture and its arrangement may also establish a hierarchy between teacher and pupils. Heavy doors and staircases between floors do not prevent cooperation between teachers on different floors, but certainly make it more difficult. Small and dirty toilets with bad locks teach many pupils that their intimate needs are not respected in school. All such experiences and uses of the school buildings can be observed and interpreted.

Thus, it is possible to use observation of lived and embodied experiences and uses of school buildings in order to acquire knowledge about educational significations. This kind of phenomenological observation is delimited by the regional world and practice of the school where the educational significations are experienced and used by different persons who work in the buildings. To support the interpretations of the observations, they must also be extended over time. The preferred kind of methodology for the study of educational significations thus seems to be some kind of field study.

Field studies also have the advantage of balancing distance with closeness. By being a stranger, the researcher has, on the one hand, a distance to the school buildings and their practice. Furthermore, the researcher explicitly distances him/herself as a result of analysing the empirical material. But by participating in the practice over a period of time, it is possible to explore the educational significations in their lived and embodied experience and use. In this methodology, there is nothing to prevent the researchers themselves from participating in the different activities in order to trace the educational significations. There is also nothing that precludes utilising conversations between different actors in the school or the initiation of conversations in connection with an ongoing activity in order to support the actors' linguistification of their experiences (Bengtsson, 2005). This methodology is thus inclusive rather than exclusive.

The life-world approach is a research approach close to practice that develops its methods based on its ontological understanding of the regional reality to be studied (Bengtsson, 2005). In the life-world approach, however, "research close to practice" does not only mean research that is carried out in the midst of practice. It is also an ontologically reflected and motivated point of view. The results of the ontological analysis of educational significations in school buildings carried out in this chapter led to the choice of the field study as an adequate method. The knowledge that in this way can be acquired about educational significations in school buildings can be expected to be of immediate practical value for teachers as well as for school architects (Bengtsson, 1993).

Acknowledgments

This chapter was part of a research project called "The signification of the physical room for learning", financially supported by the Swedish Research Council. The chapter is based on a symposium I organised at the annual conference of the Nordic Educational Research Association in Reykjavik in 2004 with contributions by Eva Alerby, Patrick Bjurström, Maj-Lis Hörnqvist and myself. I am indebted to this research group for critical comments on my paper. All photos in this chapter were taken by the author. The last photo (no. 10) is published with the permission of the boy's parents.

References

Alerby, E., Bengtsson, J., Hörnqvist, M-L & Kroksmark, T. (2002). Reflections on the Signification of Space in School from a Life-World Approach, in *Education-Line* 2002, http://www.leeds.ac.uk/educol/documents/
Asplund, G., Gahn, W., Markelius, S., Paulsson, G. Sundahl, E & Åhrén, U. (1931). *Acceptera* [Accept]. Stockholm: Bokförlagsaktiebolaget Tiden.
Bengtsson, J. (1993). Theory and Practice: two Fundamental Categories in the Philosophy of Teacher Education, *Educational Review* 45/3, 205–211.
Bengtsson, J. (ed.) (2005). *Med livsvärlden som grund. Bidrag till utvecklandet av en livsvärldsfenomenologisk ansats i pedagogisk forskning* [With the Life-World as Point of Departure]. 2nd revised edition, Lund: Studentlitteratur.
Besset, M. (1992). *Le Corbusier*. Genève: Editions d'Art Albert Skira.

Björklid, P. (2005). *Lärande och fysisk miljö. En kunskapsöversikt om samspelet mellan lärande och fysisk miljö i förskola och skola* [Learning and Physical Environment]. Stockholm: Myndigheten för skolutveckling.
Bjurström, P. (2004 a). Historisk beskrivning av skolbyggnaden [Historical Description of the School Building], Manuscript 27/10.
Bjurström, P. (2004 b). *Att förstå skolbyggnader* [To Understand School Buildings]. Doctoral thesis 2004:2. Stockholm: Royal Institute of Technology, School of Architecture.
Böhme, J. (ed.) (2009). *Schularchitektur im interdisziplinären Diskurs.* Wiesbaden: Vs Verlag.
Burke, C. & Grosvenor, I. (2003). *The School I'd Like. Children and Young People's Reflections on an Education for the 21st Century.* London: Routledge Falmer.
Cold, B. (2002). *Skolemiljø. Fire fortellinger* [School Environment. Four Narratives]. Oslo: Kommuneforlaget.
David, T. G. & Weinstein, C. S. (eds.) (1987). *Spaces for Children. The Built Environment and Child Development.* New York: Plenum Press.
Dudek, M. (2000 a). *Kindergarten Architecture. Space for the Imagination.* London: The Spon Press.
Dudek, M. (2000 b). *Architecture of Schools. The New Learning Environments.* Oxford: Architectural Press.
Eriksen, A. (1996). *Skolen som et lærested og et værested* [The School as Place for Learning and Being]. Fredrikshavn: Dafolo Forlag.
Foucault, M. (1974). *Surveiller et punir.* Paris: Gallimard.
Gitz-Johansen, T., Kampmann, J. & Kirkeby, I. M. (2001). *Samspill mellem børn og skolens fysiske ramme* [Interaction Between Children and the Physical Frames of the School]. Copenhagen: Rum Form Funktion.
Hart, S. (1993). *Frank Lloyd Wright.* London: Bison Books.
Herklint, E. (2000). *Bevarandets etiska funktioner. Relationer mellan människor, platser och hus* [The Ethical Functions of Preserving. Relationships Between People, Places and Houses]. Chalmer's University of Technology, School of Architecture.
Holm, B. (1999). Hur ska vi handla upp världens bästa skola? [How should we purchase the best school in the world?]. In O. Stahle et al., *Arkitektur och skola. Om att planera skolhus,* Stockholm: Arkus, 36–43.
Jackson, P. W. (1990). *Life in Classrooms.* New York: Teachers College Press.
Jelink, F-J & Kemnitz, H. (2003) (eds.). *Die pädagogische Gestaltung des Raums. Geschichte und Modernität.* Bad Heilbrunn: Verlag Julius Klinkhardt.
de Jong, M. (1995). Att beskriva och tolka skolbyggnadens utformning [To Describe and Interpret the Design of the School Buildings]. *Krut* 77, 44–49.

Kristenson, H. (1998). Lydnad, flit och ordning. Om 1800-talets skolbyggande [Obedience, Diligence and Order. About Buildings of Schools in the 19th Century]. In K. Dunér & T. Hall (eds.), *Den svenska staden*. Stockholm: Sveriges Radios Förlag.

Kristenson, H. (1998). Skolhuset inför ett nytt sekel [The School House Before a New Century]. In S. Å. Nilsson & L. Vinge (eds.), *Kring 1900*. Nyhamnsläge, Gyllenstiernska Krapperupsstifelsen, 274–306.

Kristenson, H. (1999). Det svenska skolhuset [The Swedish School House], *ARTES, Tidskrift för Litteratur, Konst och Musik* 25/1, 58–75.

Kristenson, H. & Balgård, S. (1995). Bygga för bildning [Building for Education], In K. Dunér & T. Hall, T. (eds.), *Svenska hus*. Stockholm, Carlssons.

Krut (1995). Special issue: The School Buildings, no 77

Krut (2003). Special issue: The Educational Room, no 112.

Lindblad, B. (1993). *Skolgården – barnets frirum. Studie av en skolgårdsmiljö betraktad ur ett utvecklingspsykologiskt perspektiv* [The School Yard – the Free Room of the Children]. Gävle: Statens institut för byggnadsforskning.

Lindholm, G. (1995). *Skolgården. Vuxnas bilder, barnets miljö* [The School Yard. Images of the Adults, the Child's Environment]. Alnarp: Movium.

Mårtensson, B. (1999). Resultatet beror på byggprocessen [The Result Depends on the Building Process], In O. Stahle et al., *Arkitektur och skola. Om att planera skolhus*. Stockholm: Arkus, 50–61.

Norberg-Schulz, C. (1980). *Genius loci. Towards a Phenomenology of Architecture*. London: Academy Editions.

Olson, L. (ed.) (1992). *Karl Johansskolan* [Karl Johansskolan]. Göteborg: Stadsdelsförvaltningen Majorna.

Olsson, T. (1995). *Skolgården. Det gränslösa uterummet* [The School Yard. The Exterior Space without Limits]. Stockholm: Liber.

Pluckrose, H. (1975). *Open School, Open Society*. London: Evans Bros.

Rosén, C-J (1995). Byggnaden som skola. Ett försök att beskriva arkitekturens pedagogiska möjligheter [The Building as School. An Essay to Describe the Educational Possibilities of Architecture], *Krut* no 77, 28–37.

Skantze, A. (1989). *Vad betyder skolhuset? Skolans fysiska miljö ur elevernas perspektiv studerad i relation till barns och ungdomars utvecklingsuppgifter* [What Does the School House Mean?]. Stockholm: Department of Education, University of Stockholm.

Skantze, A. (1995). Barns och ungdomars perspektiv [Children's and Youth's Perspective], *Krut* no 77, 10–15.

Stahle, O. et al. (1999). *Arkitektur och skola. Om att planera skolhus* [Architecture and School. On Planning School Houses]. Stockhom: Stiftelsen ARKUS.

Thiis-Evensen, T. (1987). *Archetypes in Architecture*. Oslo: Universitetsforlaget.
Törnquist, A. (2005). *Skolhus för tonåringar. Rumsliga aspekter på skolans organisation och arbetssätt* [School Houses for Teenagers]. Stockholm: Arkus.
Ulleberg, H. P. (1996). Arkitektur som makt. Skolebygget som disiplinerende materiell [Architecture as Power], *Norsk Pedagogisk Tidsskrift* 80/1, 33–41.
Werne, F. (1987). *Den osynliga arkitekturen* [The Invisible Architecture]. Gothenburg: Vinga Press.

The space of the school as a changing educational tool

Patrick Bjurström

The school building and the concept of space as a machine

In what ways can a school building be comprehended as a tool for teaching and learning? How can such a tool be improved? Must such a tool be thought of as repressive in character? Referring to John Dewey's vision of society and education (Dewey, 2004; Cremin, 1964; Hartman, 1995), I argue that the school can be transformed into a successively more democratic, more liberating institution, corresponding to the needs of children as well as democratic society. As an architect I pragmatically assume that the building, the physical frame, place and space for the teaching and learning processes, has a role to play in this context. What else would be the purpose of school building design? Here, we have a field for co-operation between teachers and architects in an attempt to better understand the nature of the school building and further develop the building, and the ways to improve it.

The building can in several ways be regarded as an educational tool. My main concern here is not with the equipment of the building although as everyone knows, a school needs good equipment, suited to the specific use of the different rooms, such as libraries, physics and chemistry laboratories, workshops and gymnasiums, as well as rooms and space for more general use. Also, my main concern here is not with the technical quality of the building although, as everyone knows, a good school needs a good climate, light and acoustics, suited to the specific and general use of rooms and space. Neither am I primarily concerned with the aesthetic quality of the building, although we have good reasons to believe (Cold, 2002) that high aesthetic quality of the school building does have an inspiring and stimulating effect on the learning process as well as a cultivating effect.

No matter how important these matters are, my main interest in this chapter follows the theory of Bill Hillier and Julienne Hanson as expressed in *The social logic of space* (Hillier & Hanson, 1984*), Space is the machine* (Hillier, 1996) and the concept of *space syntax*. Using the term *syntax,* Hillier and Hanson (1984) regard space as a language, not what is called a natural language such as English or Swedish but a "morphic language". Syntax, "the most important property of a morphic language" (p. 48), is concerned with how the entities of the language are arranged. Space syntax theory attempts to "capture the fundamental similarities and differences of real space forms in as economical a way as possible" (p. 12). The immediate outcome of space syntax analysis generally comes in the form of graphs and numbers.

According to Hillier and Hanson (Hillier & Hanson, 1984, p. ix), the most far-reaching practical effects of architecture are not "on the level of appearances" but "at the level of *space*". Hillier and Hanson's theory, an analytic theory of architecture, a theory about the spatial logic of buildings, seems particularly applicable to school buildings, as shown by de Jong (1995, 1999). As Hillier and Hanson's title *The social logic of space* implies, architecture has the capacity to do something with people. The way architecture acts is primarily by forming space. The idea that architecture has the capacity to *do*, to *act*, recurs in a similar way in Goetz (2001) with the concept of "mode d'action" of architecture.

The way parts of space are connected is, according to Hillier and Hanson, far more important in its effect than any single part. Buildings influence people, through their layout, their spatial relations, often in a hidden way. In physical terms, buildings form the conditions for human behavior and interaction. As Markus (1993), Tschumi (1996) as well as Hillier and Hanson (1984) have pointed out that this capacity of architecture is often neglected in the theory, criticism and public debate about architecture. Education is also about influencing (de Jong, 1999, p. 2).

Hillier's machine metaphor should however not be carried too far. The point is not whether a building, like a machine, contains moving parts. Neither does Hillier mean to say that a building has the capacity of a machine in the sense of changing a piece of material into something else. Buildings do affect people although not quite so literally. In elucidating Le Corbusier's famous metaphor of the house as a machine for living in, Hillier (1996) regards "the plan as an organizer of life that goes on in a building". Like a machine, a building is a system of integrated parts. In buildings, as in machines, movement is something essential. All social interaction as well as experiencing architecture requires movement.

Hillier and Hanson's theory says that for any spatial organization of a building (or indeed, an urban settlement) there is a corresponding social organization or pattern of social interaction. This view should, however, not be interpreted as deterministic (Hillier & Hanson, 1984; Hillier, 1996; de Jong, 1999). The building does not determine human social behavior, especially not on an individual level, but forms possibilities and obstacles on the level of system. What is made possible does not always become real. However, Hillier and Hanson suspect (1984; Hillier, 1996) that much malfunction of the modern built environment is caused by the ignorance of architects and planners in the field of space syntax. Hillier and Hanson even speak (1984; Hillier, 1996) of spatial and environmental "pathology".

The space of the school

Supporting our view of what essentially constitutes architecture, Tschumi (1996) opposes the conventional view of architecture as an object of contemplation, easily accessible to critical attention. Instead, he points to the role of architecture in the interaction between space and events. Architecture, in his words deals with "the movement of bodies in space" (p. 148). Is not this how people normally use and experience buildings? And is not this how we picture the interaction of children and teachers?

In buildings, entities of space are formed as rooms of different sizes, separated by boundaries such as walls, and connected by openings such as doors. The interconnection of rooms forms patterns of various shapes. Hillier (1996) uses the term *configuration*. These patterns form prerequisites for movement through the building, and for human interaction. A problem in the theory of architecture, the problem that Hillier and Hanson have aspired to solve, is to make these patterns accessible to investigation and criticism, to provide instruments for comparing the spatial pattern of one building with another.

The space syntax theory of Hillier and Hanson (1984; Hillier, 1996) offers methods to describe such patterns, and each part of them, mathematically and graphically. Hillier and others (Hanson, 1998; de Jong, 1995, 1999; Marcus, 2000) have shown how such mathematical descriptions can be interpreted and made accessible to experts and non-experts. Thus, space syntax theory has developed a vocabulary that facilitates the discussion about the spatial organization of a building, or a city. For example, some forms of spatial organization can be described as *tree-like*, others as *ringy* (figure 1). Within a spatial organization, the different spaces can be measured and compared regarding their degree of *integration*. A measurable quality of any spatial organization is its *depth*. This sort of exact description in graphs, numbers and specialized terms, has been shown to form a firm basis for a more general discussion about different building types such as houses (Hanson, 1998). In this chapter, I intend to point to the meaning of space and the use of space syntax theory in the study of school buildings. The next step would be a deeper, comparative study of Swedish school buildings as spatial systems.

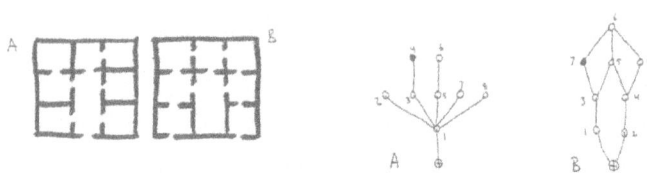

Figure 1: A simple example of space syntax analysis – two hypothetical floor plans and corresponding graphs. Depending on where the doors are placed, the same basic set of rooms can form different spatial systems such as a tree-like one (A), or a ringier one (B) (from de Jong, 1995).

Questions of power and control

In Hanson's study of homes and houses in different cultures (Hanson, 1998), spatial patterns have been interpreted as reflections of power and control, or occasionally the absence of power and control. The spatial pattern or configuration is hardly the sole instrument of power and control but can in various ways either support or undermine the structure of the organization that inhabits the buildings. Quoting Marcus (2000, p. 25), a social order is given physical expression in a spatial order, while the spatial order supports the social order. Putting it harshly, Marcus says that the spatial order is an important way for the social order to reproduce itself. Putting it more mildly, let us say that the spatial order normally supports a certain social order, even where changes do take place.

Regarding homes, Hanson writes (1998, p. 269):

> Space configurations, object arrays and people's routines can ... be decoded so that the social and symbolic information are retrieved directly from how houses are organized and used. These spatial descriptions are independent of people's experiences and feelings about their homes. They speak directly to us about how the social universe is constructed and reproduced in everyday life ...

We assume that something similar can be said about schools. And so, space syntax theory should be an interesting method in the research on school buildings. This method should, of course, not exclude other methods such as interviewing teachers and pupils about their experiences and feelings.

If the spatial pattern of a building offers social possibilities, all of these possibilities are not automatically open to everyone who enters the building. In any social setting such as a school there are always certain intentions, social codes and rules regarding the use of the building and the different rooms within it (Rapoport, 1995; Kirkeby, 2003). Some, but not all such intentions, codes and rules are written down on paper. Access to rooms is controlled by boundaries and may be accentuated by locking doors (de Jong, 1999). In some buildings the functional aims, the codes and rules of behavior are supported by the spatial organization of the building; in others they are undermined. For example, the teacher's visual control of pupils, traditionally thought of as something important, is not always supported by the spatial organization of a new school. In some buildings, there may be contradictions or "misfits", meaning that the building has a potential not permitted in its actual use. The advantage of a centrally located school library decreases if the library is seldom open.

Who sets the rules, who has control, who is permitted access to what parts of space, when and why? What activities and behavior are considered appropriate in a certain room? In almost every building there is an established social order. In most workplaces there is a boss, a formal and informal hierarchy, etc. Hillier and Hanson (1984) make an important basic distinction between the two categories of users of a building, be it private or public; *inhabitants* and *visitors*. Only the inhabitants have, in the words of Hillier and Hanson (1984, p. 184; de Jong, 1999), the power to "control the knowledge embodied in the building and its purposes".

In schools, de Jong, like Hillier & Hanson, regards teachers as "inhabitants" and children as "visitors". Following my own observations, however, in the way I interpret a school, this relationship can in some cases be turned upside down. When a new teacher enters a classroom she may find that the pupils have their own set of rules that may be in conflict with the formal rules. In such a case, the teacher becomes visitor. In other cases, in a particular classroom, some pupils are quite likely to feel themselves as inhabitants, whereas other pupils are seen as visitors. The roles of inhabitant and visitor in a school are not absolutely fixed but subject to contest and change. In fact, the democratic progress in the educational system as envisioned by Dewey (Hartman, 1995; Hartman et al. in Dewey, 2004) must include changes regarding the roles of teacher and pupil. Anyway, an abstract relationship such as between inhabitants and visitors is in any case mediated through the use of space.

My objective is not to teach teachers how to handle difficult situations. My point is simply that the same object, the same spatial organization may be regarded and used in quite different ways depending on who you are and what your interests are. For a teacher who wants to teach and a pupil who wants to learn, the school building may be experienced as a more or less efficient tool for teaching and learning. For someone who feels forced to attend school, that need not be quite the case. The question is not only one of influence but also of power and resistance.

Thomas Markus, in *Buildings and Power* (1993) sees reproducing the power of the client as a primary aim of buildings. According to Ulleberg (1996), a primary aim of schools is to foster obedience. Joel Spring (1975) as well as Foucault (Kirkeby, 2006) have regarded the school as one of society's disciplinary institutions. Officially, repression is of course not on the agenda of a modern school. Officially, the school has changed from being authoritarian to being more democratic. In the 1960s and 1970s, however, the idea of a hidden agenda in the educational system was introduced, first in the U.S. by P. Jackson, then in Sweden by D. Broady (Bjurström, 2000). One form such a hidden agenda takes may be the traditional school building, which may be regarded as resisting change.

Why should we make a connection between the idea of a hidden agenda and spatial configuration? First, because the spatial configuration is often something hardly noticed or discussed (Hillier & Hanson, 1984; Tschumi, 1996); second, because a spatial configuration tends to reflect the idea behind an organization as well as sustaining existing power relations (Hillier & Hanson, 1984; Hanson, 1998; Marcus, 2000).

Recently, this type of critique of the school and the school building has been expressed by the Danish architect Inge Mette Kirkeby, in collaboration with two educational scientists, Jan Kampmann and Thomas Gitz-Johansen (Gitz-Johansen et al., 2001; Kirkeby, 2003, 2006). Following Foucault, Kirkeby still regards the way the school controls children's physical and social behavior as an important aspect of what the school does to them. Not only in the old authoritarian days but also in a modern classroom, children are often forced to be seated, forced to face the teacher, not contact each other, and not leave the room. The school controls the social and physical energy of the children in the creation of order. The architecture and furniture are seen as instruments of such control – walls and closed or locked doors, and not least chairs. Kirkeby advocates a greater acceptance of children's needs, more liberating ways of teaching and learning, and a corresponding architecture.

However, in an analysis of three Danish schools for first and second grade pupils (Gitz-Johansen et al., 2001), the newest school (built in 1998) seems to mark a step forward, not only in aesthetic quality and symbolic meaning but also in its spatial organization, notably, the way furniture affects the use of space. As one positive example, she observes that in one classroom there are not enough chairs for all the children, which means that some of the children must do their work on the floor or must go to some other place. This is perhaps an odd example of how new forms of teaching and learning can encourage movement. It is also an example of how, in the use of space, not only a chair but the absence of a chair can function as a tool for teaching and learning.

Separation or integration

Although Dewey was neither an architect nor primarily interested in architecture, his influence can be seen indirectly in the way the typical school building has changed since the 1950s, not least in Sweden. Architects as well as teachers have seen the opportunities for educational progress through changes in school architecture. Dewey, famous for the phrase "learning by doing" had a vision of the more democratic, more integrating school as becoming more of a laboratory, less of an auditorium (Dewey, 2004, p. 73). Such a change would require more than the addition of new equipment. The change has to involve the spatial configuration of the school.

From the point of view of this chapter, our concern with space (shared with Hillier & Hanson), the process of teaching and learning is seen as a social process. Some words used by Hillier (1996) to define human social activity such as co-presence, co-absence, co-awareness, encountering, congregating, avoiding and interacting seem well suited to schools. Although we may at other times be interested in what goes on inside someone's brain, this is not the primary aspect of the learning process here. Neither do we think that one person reading a book poses much of a spatial problem. In fact, teaching and learning processes, involving one or more persons, can and do take place in almost any kind of environment. A school, however, as a place for social processes of learning, usually involving large numbers of people, poses interesting spatial problems for architects to solve in co-operation with users and others (project managers, consulting engineers, etc.). Essentially, if we accept Hillier's theory, this is what school design is about.

The two categories of people, whether they are called inhabitants and visitors (Hillier & Hanson, 1984; de Jong, 1996), or staff and pupils, can usually be sorted into a number of subcategories and down to individuals, regarding age, ability and sex, subjects and specialties of teachers and other staff, etc. Interaction between these, in space and time, as individuals and groups is a part of the social process of teaching and learning. Different teaching strategies may determine the size of groups, duration of groups, the social composition of groups and the hierarchy of groups. With co-presence and co-awareness in a room as basis, social interaction within and between groups, also involving power relations, may be supported or undermined by the spatial organization. Obviously, the sizes, equipment, technical and aesthetic quality of rooms form possibilities and obstacles for different forms of teaching and learning. Depending on previous knowledge and imaginative thinking, teachers and pupils are more or less able to see the possibilities and to use the rooms and equipment.

According to Hillier, however, the order or configuration of rooms is a most important, although perhaps hidden factor, regarding the social use of the building. As an example, shown by de Jong (1995), in one spatial pattern, teachers and other staff are likely to form one cohesive social group, in another spatial pattern they are more likely to form several smaller groups. As another example, the location of a school library to some extent determines its use.

A key concept in the development of the Swedish school as in the philosophy of Dewey is *integration*. Incidentally, perhaps, the term integration is also much used by Hillier in space syntax theory. For Dewey, the term is positive, used by Hillier (1996) it becomes more technical; like air temperature it is something that can be measured and can contain useful information.

Hartman differentiates between a *separating* and an *integrating* perspective and reflects on the effects on the organization of social groups, on knowledge, time and physical space (Hartman, 1995, p. 168–169). In my condensed interpretation, Hartman makes the following distinctions:

• *social organization*: the separating perspective says parents should have the opportunity to choose the school suited to the special ability of the child. The integrating perspective says all children should go to the same kind of school.

• *teacher – pupil relation*: according to the separating perspective, the teacher plans and conducts the work. According to the integrating perspective, teacher and pupils plan together; the nature of the work and individual interests and needs of pupils are taken into account; the pupils often work in flexible groups.

• *knowledge organization*: the separating perspective regards knowledge as a firm substance to be transmitted to the pupils. Theoretical knowledge is considered to be more valuable than practical or aesthetic knowledge. The integrating perspective regards knowledge as something changing, it stresses the activity of the pupil in the learning process and says the aim of teaching should be to teach pupils how to learn.

• *time organization:* according to the separating perspective, the school day should follow a strict timetable, with strict division between class and recess. According to the integrating perspective, the use of time should be flexible, depending on the type of work.

• *spatial organization*: the separating perspective states that the school building should separate different programmes and classes and should contain mostly classrooms and have little space for common use. The integrating perspective states that the spatial design should facilitate contact between different groups and classes. There should be much space for common use as well as for individual and group work.

The view of the spatial organization of the building not only runs parallel with the views of social and work relations, of knowledge and the use of time. It is quite possible though not always certain that a spatial analysis using Hillier's method would confirm our more spontaneous opinion when we regard a particular school as integrating from the viewpoint of Dewey/Hartman. In a short discussion about schools, traditional and open-plan schools and the idea of

The space of the school 43

"liberalization of space" Hillier & Hanson (1984) point out that "buildings are rarely what they seem". In space syntax theory, buildings are analyzable. One objective of such an analysis is to point out such consequences regarding human behavior that may not be fully clear either to the architect or planner or to the users.

If we adopt the integrating perspective, and we regard the school building, from the perspective of spatial organization, as a tool for teaching and learning, it should function as a tool for social integration. In Sweden and other countries, we can observe an ongoing change, a transformation of school buildings (Löwenhielm, 1999; Bjurström, 2000, 2002, 2003) in this direction. A new type of layout plan supersedes the traditional classroom and corridor. The traditional classroom, which is still predominant in existing schools, is a room of about 60 square meters, for one teacher and 25 or 30 pupils (figure 2). This traditional classroom has only one door, which connects it to a corridor. In some new schools and renovated schools, there are very few such rooms. Instead, rooms are of various sizes, interconnected in various ways. Glazed walls and open doors are other means to further counteract the stuffiness of the old type of school. The former corridors are largely integrated as space for teaching and learning. Often, a unit is formed for 75 or 80 pupils and 6 – 8 teachers and the rooms for such a unit also include workspace for teachers. Examples are the renovated school Futurum, and the new schools Gröna Dalen (in translation: "Green Valley"), Trädgårdsstad (in translation: "Garden Town"; figure 3) and Fryxell School (Bjurström, 2002, 2003).

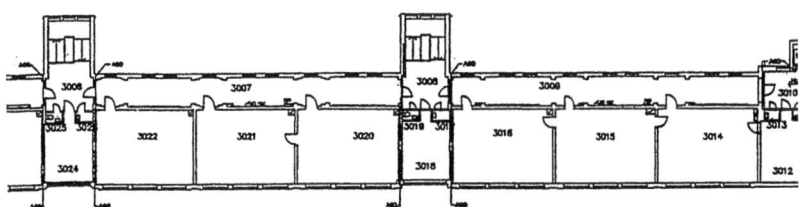

Figure 2: Norra Örnäs School, Luleå (Architect: John Berglund, 1952). Part of 3rd floor. The traditional layout of corridor and row of identical classrooms remains. The doors that interconnect some classrooms are a recent change.

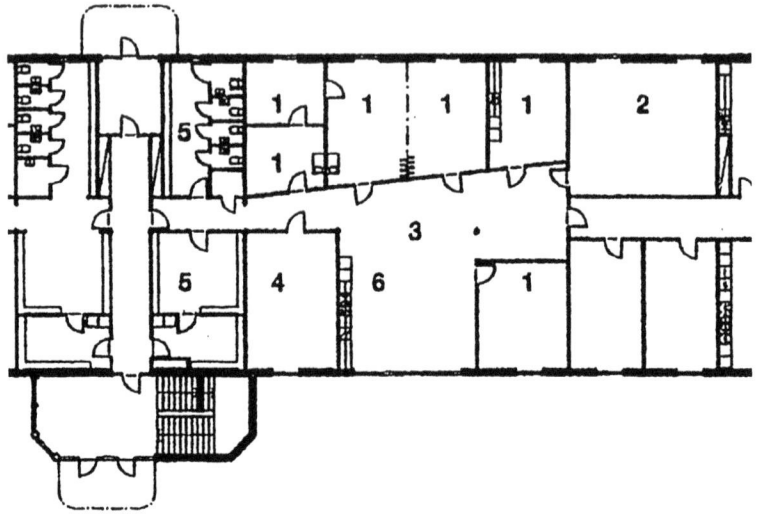

Figure 3: "Garden Town School", Botkyrka (Architect: Gösta Öhman, 2002). Part of ground floor. Within each unit for 75 pupils, there is a varied set of rooms.
1. *Classroom*
2. *Classroom/ Laboratory*
3. *Multi-use room*
4. *Teachers' room*
5. *Cloakroom*
6. *Kitchen*

The need to analyze and evaluate the changing school building

In terms of spatial configuration (Hillier, 1996), even small changes such as opening up walls and putting in doors between classrooms result in a significant change, making the pattern more ringy. Replacing the row of classrooms with clusters of interconnected rooms increases the depth of the configuration. Further research on spatial organization of schools is expected to more specifically reveal differences in character between different school buildings, and the consequences on the processes of teaching and learning.

There is a need to analyze and evaluate the ongoing change in school buildings, in Sweden and in other countries, not least in terms of their spatial organization. In practice, such evaluation is taking place as a by-product of the inspections made by the National Agency for Education in our schools (e.g.

The space of the school

Skolverket, 2003). For our purposes, these inspections are not enough, lacking as they are as far as theory of the social and educational meaning of architecture is concerned. In such a project, however, we cannot take for granted what should be meant by teaching and learning and what should be meant as the primary purposes of teaching and learning. Above, we have, referring to Dewey (2004), and to Hartman (1995) touched upon opposing views of such matters as theoretical or practical knowledge, of acquiring specific pieces of knowledge or learning to learn. A current debate in Sweden concerns the purpose of the school as well as teaching and learning methods. According to official documents (Lpo 94, etc.), the school is important as a place where we learn how to relate and co-operate with other people. According to conservative critics (Enkvist, 2003, p. 8), the adequate, traditional aim of building up knowledge has been devaluated through the efforts of "certain political interests and certain groups in the academic world" (author's translation).

In this debate, the progressive philosophy of Dewey is sometimes transformed into a caricature. While Dewey (2004) highlighted the importance of active, individual learning and deplored the traditional classroom situation where pupils are passive receivers of information, this does not mean that the pupils should be left to do whatever they want. Dewey also emphasized the importance of the teacher whose mastery of subject matter is as important as teaching ability. To the extent that the interface between teacher and pupil is a part of the spatial organization of the building, the building should be formed as a support.

In the classroom as well as in society in general, we can, however, observe an erosion of the power of visible authorities. The integrating perspective involves a redistribution of power, of control, from teacher to pupil. This change does not necessarily relieve pressure on the pupil. As Basil Bernstein puts it (Gitz-Johansen et al., 2001), the new educational practices are simply less visible.

Officially, as a part of an ongoing change in Sweden and other countries (Gitz-Johansen et al., 2001), the pupil is given more responsibility for his/her own learning. The chance of failure should, however, not be excluded. For a teacher, to simply let the children slip out of the classroom, to whatever space and whatever activity they may think up can be a frustrating experience. What architecture does, without being a major force, is to assist in a redistribution of power, control and responsibility. The increased transparency in modern architecture, including schools, by means of glazed walls and open doors (Bjurström, 2003), may counteract the sense of social dispersion and balance the teacher's loss of control.

In the pessimistic, highly critical interpretation by Markus (1993), the disappearance of the corridor in the new schools is not a step forward. Markus discusses control and surveillance as characteristic of today's society. The corridor was in fact, he claims, for the children "the freest and most programmed space" (Markus 1993, p. 94). He regards the open-plan school as modeled like a type of modern office, "the electronic office", where material articulation of power has become more subtle and despite the egalitarian rhetoric of flexibility, privacy and space for relative autonomy have disappeared".

Educators, planners and architects should listen to the warning. The open-plan school of the 1960s or 1970s was not the optimal solution. Neither is the electronic office the best model for an environment for children, nor should the task of teachers be mainly control and surveillance. Returning to the more optimistic Dewey, his model for the school was not the electronic office (Dewey, 2004). Following his idea of the school as a more democratic, more liberating, more integrating institution, the task of teachers should not be that of surveillance and control.

We may agree with Foucault in regarding the old familiar school as typically a tool for the exercise of discipline. With the new school, new possibilities open up. While possibly turned into a tool for surveillance and control, there is also the possibility for better opportunities, for new forms of interaction and co-operation between teachers and pupils. With the advancement in architectural method, specifically in the technique of space syntax analysis, the capacity of architects to predict the possible social outcome of layout plans is expected to improve. How the possibilities offered through the architecture of the school will actually be utilized is normally not for the architect to determine.

The new spatial organization of the school must not be regarded, or designed, just as an end in itself. It may prove to be an interesting tool for teaching and learning as part of a new strategy, in the interest of individuals as well as society. The use of such a tool, however, also requires new forms of teaching involving the education of teachers. In my work as architect and my study of architecture and of school buildings in particular, I have come across a range of ideas and theories regarding the nature of buildings and the relation between buildings and people. For an architect, every process of planning and building turns out to be more or less complicated, but the nature of the goal may still seem rather uncomplicated. The goal, whether we design a house, an apartment building, an office building or a school, is about problem solving and improvement, with respect to both user and client as well as society in general and the culture of architecture.

Acknowledgments

This chapter is part of a research project called "The signification of the physical room for learning", financially supported by the Swedish Research Council. The chapter is based on a symposium at the annual conference of the Nordic Educational Research Association in Reykjavik in 2004 with contributions by

Eva Alerby, Jan Bengtsson, Maj-Lis Hörnqvist and myself. I am indebted to this research group for critical comments on this chapter.

References

Bjurström, P. (2000). *Att anpassa skolbyggnader till nya arbetsformer* [Adapting School Buildings to New Forms of Teaching and Learning]. Stockholm: KTH.
Bjurström, P. (2002). *Skolbyggnad och arbetslag. En fallstudie i Futurum* [School Building and Working Team. A Case Study]. Stockholm: KTH.
Bjurström, P. (2003). Pedagogik och arkitektur för en orolig tid [Education and Architecture for a troubled time]. *Arkitektur* 8/03.
Cold, B. (2002). *Skolemiljø, fire fortellinger* [The School Environment, Four Visions]. Oslo: Kommuneforlaget, Norsk Form.
Cremin, A. (1964). *The Transformation of the School.* New York: Vintage Books.
Dewey, J., (2004). *Individ, skola och samhälle* [Individual, School and Society, with introduction by Hartman S., Lundgren, U. P. & Hartman, R. M.]. Stockholm: Natur och kultur.
Enkvist, I. (ed.) (2003). *Skolan – ett svenskt högriskprojekt* [The Swedish School – a Hazardous Project]. Stockholm: Gidlunds förlag.
Gitz-Johansen, T. Kampmann, J., & Kirkeby, I. M. (2001). *Samspil mellem børn og skolens fysiske ramme* [Interplay between Children and the Physical Frame of the School]. Copenhagen: Rum, Form, Funktion.
Goetz, B. (2001). *La dislocation, architecture et philosophie* [Dislocation, Architecture and Philosophy]. Paris: Les Èditions de la Passion.
Hanson, J. (1998). *Decoding Homes and Houses.* Cambridge, U. K.: Cambridge University Press.
Hartman, S. (1995). *Lärares kunskap* [The Knowledge of Teachers]. Linköping: University of Linköping.
Hillier, B. (1996). *Space is the Machine.* Cambridge, U.K.: Cambridge University Press.
Hillier, B. & Hanson, J. (1984). *The Social Logic of Space.* Cambridge, U.K.: Cambridge University Press.
de Jong, M. (1995). Att beskriva och tolka skolbyggnaders utformning [To Describe and Interpret the Shape of School Buildings]. *Krut* 77.
de Jong, M. (1999). *Space-Syntax as an Approach to Analyse Educational Buildings and Other Environments for Children.* Paper, annual conference of the Nordic Educational Research Association, 1999. Copenhagen
Kirkeby, I. M. (2003). Det adfærdsregulerende rum. Kontrol, delegation og kode [Space that Regulates Behaviour. Control, Delegation, Code]. *Nordisk Arkitekturforskning* 3/03.

Kirkeby, I. M. (2006). *Skolen finder sted* [The school takes place]. Hørsholm, Denmark: Statens Byggeforskningsinstitut.

Läroplan Lpo 94, *1994 års läroplan för det obligatoriska skolväsendet, förskoleklassen och fritidshemmet, med reviderande förordning 1998-06-11* [Curriculum from 1994 for the Compulsory School System, the Pre-School Class and the Leisure-time Centre]. Stockholm: The Ministry of Education.

Löwenhielm, G. (1999). Rum för en ny skola. In Stahle, O., (ed.) *Arkitektur och skola: om att planera skolhus* [Architecture and School: Planning School Buildings]. Stockholm: Byggförlaget, 8–19.

Marcus, L. (2000). *Architectural Knowledge and Urban Form.* Stockholm: KTH.

Markus, T. (1993). *Buildings and Power. Freedom and Control in the Origin of Modern Building types.* London and New York: Routledge.

Rapoport, A. (1995). *The Meaning of the Built Environment.* Tucson: University of Arizona Press.

Skolverket (The National Agency for Education) (2003). *Utbildningsinspektion i grundskolan Futurum* [Educational Inspection in the School Futurum]. Dnr 53-2003:1825. Stockholm.

Spring, J. (1975). *A Primer of Libertarian Education.* New York: Free Life Editions.

Tschumi, B. (1996). *Architecture and Disjunction.* Cambridge, Mass.: MIT Press.

Ulleberg, H. P. (1996). Arkitektur som makt – skolebygget som disiplinerende mode [Architecture as Agent of Power – the School Building as Disciplinarian Model]. *Norsk Pedagogisk Tidsskrift* 1/1996.

Architecture, pedagogy and children
The intersection between different action programs in school

Thomas Gitz-Johansen, Jan Kampmann and Inge Mette Kirkeby

Until recently, research on school architecture has been dominated by quantitative research in the school environment. In this body of research, the focus has largely been on physical factors such as air particles, light, noise, durability of materials and their relation to the health and wellbeing of the persons working and studying in school, for example, investigating the effect of daylight on student performance quantified by means of test scores (Loisos et al., 1999) or studying how the schoolwork of children is affected by short-term electrostatic particle filtration (Wargocki & Wyon, 2008). Also, the question of the impact of school buildings on pupils and their learning has been investigated in numerous research projects. Especially after the first wave of open-plan schools constructed in the 1970s, a number of research projects focused on the interaction between school buildings and pedagogy, often quantified in a few parameters (reviews of several research projects in: Weinstein, 1979; Kampmann, 1994; Earthman & Lemasters, 1997).

However, everyday life inside school buildings and in their surroundings is not just a one-way relationship, where children and teachers are influenced by their physical surroundings. Just as physical space influences the people who populate schools, children and teachers do things with the physical space as they incorporate the physical surroundings into their daily activities.

Educational studies have long ago abandoned the mechanistic view of education which views school and education as a black box that produces output in the form of qualifications (Young, 1971; Morrow & Torres, 1995; Kampmann, 2007). A wide range of qualitative studies recognise schools as sites of interaction and negotiation between teachers and children (Jackson, 1968; Delamont, 1976 & 1984; Woods, 1983; Hammersley & Woods, 1984; McLaren, 1998; Gordon, Holland & Lahelma, 2001) and between children themselves (LeCompte & Preissle, 1992; Thorne, 1993; Deegan, 1996; Connolly, 1998; Andersen & Kampmann, 2002). In these studies, schooling is not just seen as a matter of transmission of scholarly knowledge, but also as a matter of inclusion and exclusion, peer-group interaction, identity formation and numerous other forms of activities and processes. However, the vast majority of these studies are characterised by the near total invisibility of the physical frames, which is a dimension of all schooling and indeed of all social life. This omission is perhaps not surprising as most social science has concerned itself with social interaction in relation to historical, economic or cultural contexts, rather than in relation to a spatial context (Latour 1992; Lefebvre, 1991). Perhaps this tendency to overlook physical space has been furthered by the turn towards text, discourse and signs in social science – the so-called 'linguistic turn' (Rorty, 1992; Paget 1995), which has given predominance to the symbolic aspects of social life and largely tended to neglect its physical aspects.

As a consequence, most studies of schools can be divided into a largely quantitative body of literature, which ignores social life, and a largely qualitative body of literature, which ignores physical space. The intention of this chapter is to attempt to bridge the gap between social interaction and physical space in schools by developing an approach that can incorporate both social and physical dimensions in the analysis. To this end, the chapter will explore the somewhat broad question of the interaction of the different human (teachers and children) and non-human (buildings and furniture) actors in school. The more specific focus will be on how children's possibilities for participating in the school day is framed by the architectural and pedagogical dimensions of schooling and also how children's participation is furthered or hindered by the architectural and pedagogical context. As an analytical concept, which can be applied to architecture, pedagogy and children, 'programme' will be suggested.

The study

The study that is forming the basis of this chapter was the result of cooperation between researchers from architecture and childhood studies and educational studies. The aim of the study has been to combine the perspectives from these disciplines in order to study child/teacher/space relations while crossing the boundaries between different academic traditions. The study has used different qualitative methods for a comparative case study of three schools from different periods, with different architectural styles and with different pedagogical traditions. In this chapter, we have renamed the three schools with names that describe their architectural style: 'The Comb School', 'the Common Room School' and 'the Integrated House'. As we were especially interested in the early years of schooling, we have chosen to work with the first three years of primary school where the children are between six and ten years of age.

Methodologically, we have emphasised the use of a range of qualitative methods to produce different perspectives of the space/teacher/child interaction (Jørgensen & Kampmann, 2001; Freeman & Mathison, 2009):

The architectural perspective: to deepen the insight into the relationship between architecture, pedagogy and children, the schools were observed using ethnographic observation, which has been used by other researchers to investigate the relation between children and physical space in school settings (Skantze, 1989; Itoh, 2001). In the architectural observation, two ways of observing were employed: the first kind of observation was a study of children's and adults' ongoing activities and their relations to the physical surroundings. In the second kind of observation, the researcher (who is trained as an architect) made an analysis of the building itself where prior knowledge of the design process was used to 'read' the ideas and intentions that are materialised in the building. By putting herself in the designing architect's place the architect-researcher attempted to uncover the ideas about the activities and social life intended to take place in the school; in fact, to uncover the intentions built into the building and which will persist over time independently of the presence of the architect who designed it.[1]

The professional perspective: another method emphasised the teachers' perspective on and use of the physical space in the schools. Here, we used semi-structured qualitative interviews to elucidate how teachers understand the role of the layout of the physical classroom (Kvale, 2007). Also, we used classroom observation (Walford, 2008) to capture how teachers in practice worked with the different classroom architectures to support their pedagogical praxis.

The child perspective: following the arguments of the so-called new sociology of childhood (James & Prout, 1990; Qvortrup, et al.; 1994, Corsaro, 1997), we have given a high priority to capturing the perspective of the children in school. As some of the children in the study were as young as six years, we deemed it inappropriate to use ordinary interview-methods that may work well with adults but rarely make much sense to young children and do not match their ways of expressing themselves (Kampmann, 1998). Accordingly, we combined observation with two interview techniques, which are suitable for children and for the study of how children perceive and interact with physical space. One technique, derived from the discipline of human geography, is called mental mapping (Solomon, 1978). Here, we invited the children to draw a map of the school as seen from above and to indicate on the map which place they liked the best and which they liked the least. Apart from using the maps as a source of information in themselves, we used them as a focus point for interviews with the children, where we asked the children to talk about the maps they had drawn of the school. After the interviews, we invited the children to be our guides on a tour around the school so that they could tell us what they did and where and why they did it there. This interview method is adapted from the so-called life-style interview, which has been especially developed for interviewing children (Andenæs 1991; Haavind 1987). By combining these methods, we gained an insight into children's own perspectives on the physical space in school and into their articulation of very different spatial needs.

---

1 A conceptual outcome of this way of "reading" the architecture was the construction of a model in which physical space is divided into five different aspects or perspectives on space: social space, activity space, behaviour regulating space, space as a conveyor of meaning and tuned space as a conveyor of atmosphere (Kirkeby, 2006).

Action programs

In our attempt to discuss the interaction between architecture, pedagogy and children – three apparently very different kinds of actors – we needed an analytical concept that could apply to both buildings and objects on the one hand and to people and their activities on the other. Also, we had an analytical interest in how a building may support – or obstruct – the pedagogical program. In the word program, the prefix 'pro' (before) indicates something to come. It communicates something intentional. For instance, a teacher can be said to have a program containing the pedagogical intentions for the teaching. Program is also a meaningful concept in the field of architecture. In the design process, the program for future use is considered, and when the building is finished this program is built into the building. Hence, the program concept refers to the intentions and directedness that is a part of human actions (practice) but also of the material products of human actions (objects). Our use of the program concept is indebted to Bruno Latour who, in recent decades, has concerned himself with how things and physical surroundings are co-actors in our social life.

Latour's point is that physical objects and human actors should not necessarily be conceptualised differently. Physical objects can to a large extent perform activities, which could also have been performed by people – in Latour's terms, the physical objects become social agents in line with human social agents. For an example, one can look at Latour's description of the door closer, which is a mechanical device that makes a door close gently after it has been opened by a person. A door closer is a technical aid, a 'non-human'. The door closer has taken over the function of doorkeeper to ensure that the door is closed gently every time it has been opened, which otherwise would have been carried out by a human doorkeeper. In this light, the door closer can be seen as a hybrid, a thing that ensures the completion of an 'action program'. Engineers, architects and designers thus incorporate their intentions and ideas as action programs, which are built into their designs (Latour, 1992, p. 227ff).

Another relevant concept that we borrow from Latour is the idea of a built-in reader or built-in user. Latour likens physical objects to written texts. He discusses how all texts incorporate a built-in reader – the one to whom the text is implicitly speaking (ibid, p. 237). In the same way, we can speak of built-in user in architecture; certain actions and practices are more or less consciously pre-supposed by the designers of buildings and other physical objects. For instance, a kitchen is designed around certain presuppositions of how the users will act when they prepare food.

However, when it comes to producers of physical objects, they may not necessarily have the same intentions and act the same way as those presupposed built-in users envisioned and incorporated into the artefacts: "There might be an enormous gap between the prescribed user and the user-in-the-flesh" (ibid, p. 237). For example, the user of a door that has been fitted with a door closer could prefer the door open rather than closed and put a door jam under the door to ensure that it does not shut anyway. In this way, one can talk about the establishment of an anti-program; a program that obstructs the original program. What is called a program and an anti-program always depends on the point of view from which the programs are viewed. One could argue that the door closer represents an anti-program to an *open door program*. Latour defines programs and anti-programs as: "Each device anticipates what other actors, humans or nonhumans, may do (programs of action), but these anticipated actions may not occur because those other actors have different programs – anti-programs from the point of view of the first actor. Hence the artefact becomes the front line of a controversy between programs and anti-programs" (Latour, 1999, p. 309). As will be elaborated later, what constitutes a program and an anti-program also depends on who has the power to define the appropriate program.

In the following, we will, inspired by Latour, use the term program as an analytical concept in investigating how pedagogy, children and architecture interact. Furthermore, we will incorporate a discussion of anti-programs and distinguish between 'built-in users' and 'users-in-the-flesh' or actual users.

The architectural programs

As mentioned above, our study included The Comb School, the Common Room School and the Integrated House. The three schools are clearly very different with respect to their pedagogical and architectural programs and thus with respect to the built-in users (teachers and pupils) embedded in these programs. In the following we will identify and discuss the architectural programs of the three schools in the study, and then proceed with an analysis of how architecture and pedagogy both seem to cooperate and work against each other in the schools. Later in the chapter, we will discuss how also children have their own programs or anti-programs!

The Comb School was built in 1968. Long, one-storey high buildings with classrooms and subject rooms are organised along a central corridor (hence the resemblance to a comb). Each classroom is organised quite traditionally with rows of tables for two pupils facing a teacher's desk, giving the teacher a good view of the class and giving the children a clear view of the teacher and the blackboard behind the teacher's desk. The school administration is located away from the classrooms, creating a physical and symbolic distance between the head of the school/administration and children. This effect is strengthened by the fact that the windows of the administration are transparent from inside only, creating a one-way mirror and the ability to observe without being observed.

An interpretive reading of the school building suggests that the dominant program is traditional with a relatively clear distinction between teachers and children, teacher-centred teaching (lecturing) and with the pupils working alone or in pairs rather than engaging in group work.

The Common Room School was built in 1974. It is organised with a number of single-storey high sections, each containing a common room and a number of classrooms clustered around it. The overall impression is of a small community with a common meeting-place, much like a market place or a village square. Clearly, the school should be experienced as a friendly, inviting and informal place, which shares characteristics with the housing area around the school rather than attempts to stage the school as a formal institution. Inside the classrooms, the tables and chairs are organised in small groups so that four or more children can sit around the same table facing each other. In the corner is a sofa to be used for reading and relaxing. The interior of the classrooms reflects the program of the school as such: to create a homely and relaxed atmosphere and a sense of community between the children. A small teacher's room is placed inside each building so that during breaks teachers are not far from the children, but still in a separate room (child-adult boundaries are still kept in place).

The Integrated House was built in 1998 as an additional and separate section to another school. In the two previous examples, the schooling and caretaking functions are separated as classrooms and day-care rooms located in different parts of the building. The Integrated House, however, was build with the intention of integrating functions rather than separating them.

The same rooms are used for teaching the main part of the day and as day-care facilities in the morning and the afternoon, and the building signals and facilitates an integration of teaching and learning.

In the centre of the building is a large common room, which includes an open kitchen, and a sofas complete with a fireplace. There is access to a spacious, light room, which can be used as a stage, for acting, playing, teaching dance, music and a range of other activities.

Inside the classrooms (which, as mentioned, double as day-care rooms) the children can choose to either sit on the floor with a small table on their lap or they can choose to stand or sit at high tables with space for four or five children. In the corner is a secluded area with bookcases and a sofa. Here, the children can spend time alone or in small groups reading or chatting quietly. Thus, the interior of the building is characterised by integration of function but also by flexibility, as the many nooks and corners can be used as small working areas and movable screens can be used to shape and reshape the physical space. The program of the building could be called 'integration and flexibility'; a program that seeks to integrate the different functions and activities in the everyday life

Architecture, pedagogy and children

in school and to create flexibility in the use of physical space to accommodate changing and evolving teaching activities.

The built-in program of the three schools is clearly influenced by the different pedagogical ideals, which have characterised the periods in which they were planned and built. This creates different physical environments for the teachers and children to act in. As will be described below, the physical structure of the schools sometimes supports the programs teachers and children want to carry out, and at other times the programs of architecture and people, respectively, is more conflicting.

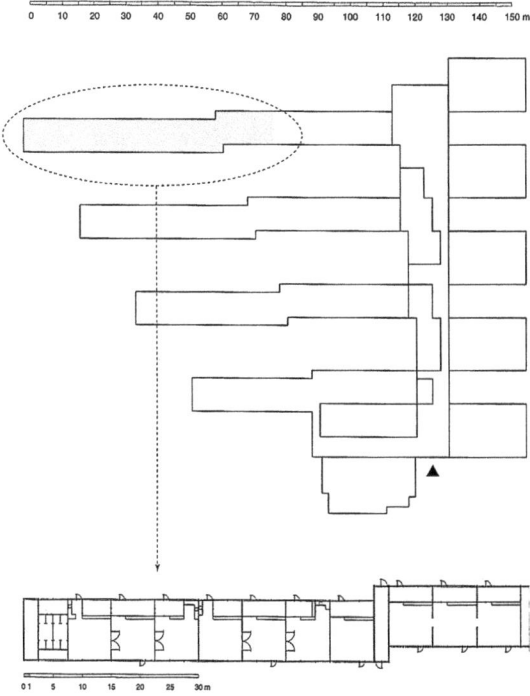

Figure 1: The comb school, plan. Entrance to each classroom, from outside to a smaller area. Today, often in use as cloakroom.

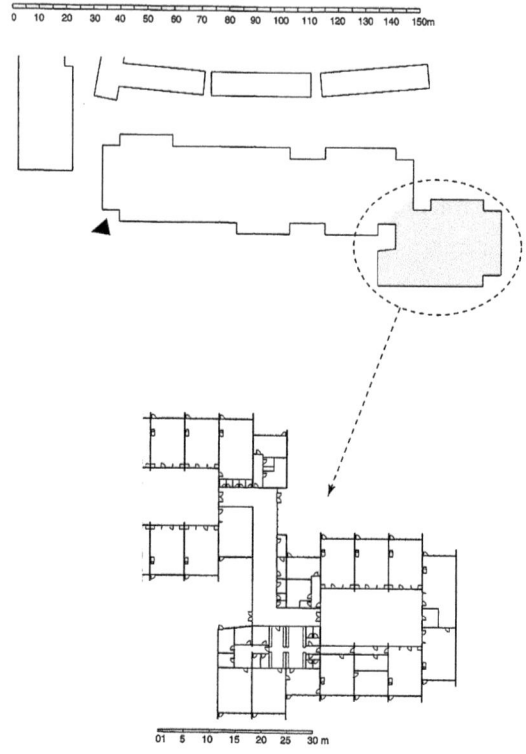

Figure 2: The common room school, plan. Classrooms centred around a common room.

Architecture, pedagogy and children 57

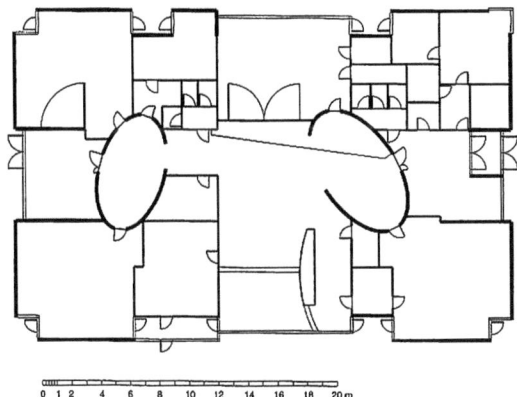

Figure 3: The integrated house, plan. The oval shaped areas giving access to different rooms are conical with skylight.

Built-in use and actual use

As described above, the schools were designed to support a specific practice according to different pedagogical ideals and thus with different 'built-in users'. However, pedagogical ideals change, and teachers do not always decipher or wish to comply with the intentions inscribed in the architecture. Also, practical circumstances may conflict with the original intentions behind the architecture (for instance, more students than originally intended may be put into a classroom). Thus, the architectural program and the teaching which actually takes place may be two different things, although they will never be completely isolated from each other as teaching always takes place somewhere and in relation to physical surroundings.

Comb School is designed so that the classrooms are connected by a long, covered pergola. Each classroom is connected to the pergola by a smaller antechamber. The antechambers were originally (in the 1960s) designed to function as a relief for the main classroom as well. Probably, the idea behind the antechambers was that smaller groups of pupils could work here undisturbed by and not disturbing what goes on in the main classroom. However, the teachers did not seem to make use of this built-in possibility, and many of the small rooms were used for storage and as a cloakroom. Only once did we see an assistant teacher sitting with a pupil for additional teaching. This was on a grey autumn day and the room was actually a bit cold – but that problem could have been solved if there had been any interest in utilising the room's potential, and if the teachers had been willing or able to read the program of the building. Instead, the teachers kept all children in the main classroom and left the smaller room empty during most lessons. At the same time, we overheard teachers complain about the lack of space. Hence, sometimes the architectural program is seems to offer possibilities that the actual pedagogical practice does not utilise. The function as storage and cloakroom became an anti-program to the built-in program, which may have been letting smaller groups of children work in the antechamber. Here, we learn that the architectural program may provide frames for and encourage a specific pedagogical program, but it cannot force a specific behaviour onto teachers who will use rooms and objects according to their own interpretation of the architecture.

The Common Room School was established in the 1970s and reflected that era's pedagogical interest in open-plan architecture instead of long rows of locked classrooms. This physical openness is meant to support combined work processes, which include numerous activities and various groupings of children and teachers. As described above, in the Common Room School, the classes are assembled around a common room. Between the classes and the common room there are three folding doors, which makes it possible to create a semi-open environment where activities in the classroom can be connected with those out in the common room. However, it was clear that the pedagogical practice we observed did not utilise this built-in opportunity to open up the environments, as tables, shelves and other furniture were piled up in front of the doors. At the same time, we observed how the teachers were trying to create a more project-oriented and differentiated style of teaching, and they struggled to get the physical environment to support this pedagogy. After making the teachers aware that the furniture was blocking some possibilities for reducing the amount of traditional class teaching, something interesting happened in that they could now see some new possibilities in the building. When we visited the school a year later, we were stopped by a teacher who explained that *now* they opened the wide doors when they needed to use the common room to have space enough for several activities at the same time and they had realised that the furniture preventing full use of the doors acted as an anti-program. In other words, they had revised the actual use of the physical space in a way that enabled them to make use of the support the building was designed to give, i.e. the teachers adapted their actual use to the built-in use when they deciphered the intentions built into the architecture.

The recently built Integration House was designed to follow a contemporary ideal of differentiated teaching, where pupils with different needs are taught at the same time in the same class and where the teaching is differentiated to meet their individual needs. Also, the older pedagogical ideal of keeping activities separate (which characterised the Comb School) were replaced by an ideal of integrating activities; the building was designed to support interdisciplinarity and a loosening of the traditional curricular structure. 'Active participation' rather than 'receptive learning' was supported. It was apparent that traditional class teaching, where all the pupils sit in the same position facing the teacher and blackboard and where the pupils are expected to learn the same thing at the same time and at the same speed was *not* the built-in ideal. The furniture and the arrangement of the classrooms meant that the children could move around and work with different tasks in changing groups and even take breaks if they felt they needed it. Firstly, there are high tables, so the children can choose between standing and sitting on the high stools and they also had the option of sitting on the floor and using low floor desks. Secondly, there were not enough stools for all the children to sit at the desks at the same time. During our fieldwork in the school, the program of the building seemed largely to support the style of teaching that took place, which was often organised as group work and often utilised the possibilities of creating a differentiated room with possibilities for children working in relative separation on different tasks. The apparent coordination between the pedagogical program and the architectural program can be explained by the building being relatively new (only about 4 years old at the time of the study) which makes likely a certain level of concordance between the built-in programme in the building and pedagogical ideals of the actual user.

Above, we have discussed how school buildings contain built-in action programs that facilitate certain types of pedagogical programs and thus act as anti-program to other types of pedagogical programs. We have also shown how the actual pedagogical use of the school buildings not only conformed to the programs built into the physical space; the architecture and objects were (especially in the two oldest schools) interpreted and used by the teachers in ways that made other practices possible and in ways that overlooked or ignored certain possibilities afforded by the architecture.

In the following, we will further explore the interplay between pedagogy and architecture, but this time our analysis will focus on the pedagogical programs and their utilisation of physical space.

The pedagogical programs

In the world of day-care institutions, the Italian so-called Reggio Emilia pedagogy has contributed substantially to an increased interest in seeing the physical space as what they term "the third teacher" with reference to its potential for supporting the pedagogical intentions and practice of the staff (Kinney & Wharton, 2008; Kampmann, 1998). This expresses the realisation that physical space is used in different ways as a pedagogical tool, or, put another way, the physical space is incorporated in the pedagogical program. The following two examples illustrate how different programs interplay. First an excerpt from a fieldwork diary from our study:

> The time is a little over 10 am and class 1.D. is assembled in the classroom. The children are sitting 2 and 2 at a total of 8 tables. There are no mattresses or cushions in the room. The teacher begins by shushing the children to be quiet. Then they practice letters and sound. The children have to say different syllables in chorus. Two of the boys in the class are not facing the board. One teacher is up at the board teaching while the other is sitting at a table between two boys who are usually disruptive in class. The class is looking in a book, talking about the pictures and reading the text. The teacher is at the front asking questions that the pupils have to answer, and the pupils have to read aloud from their book. Meanwhile the teacher attempts to quieten those who are talking together and regulate those who refuse to sit still or is not paying attention. (...) The boy I am sitting with is consequently not following what is happening on the board, but is sitting and playing with various things. The teacher regularly comments that the boy is not concentrating, which gains his attention for a short time before he resumes looking into the distance or begins playing with something or other. At one point he gets up and goes over to a boy at another table, and the teacher who is sitting down in the classroom gets him to sit down. It seems that an important part of the assistant teacher's role is to help regulate the children's movements, noise and attention. There are 5 girls in the class and they follow pretty much everything that goes on up at the blackboard, while the attention is far less directed towards the blackboard amongst the 12 boys. It is not because they are messing about, being noisy or naughty, it is just that their attention is elsewhere. The teacher suggests that they are clearly bored when they aren't following what is going on. (Comb School)

This arrangement of two-pupil tables, which partly keeps the children's attention directed towards the blackboard and partly keeps the children separated into manageable units, is well-known. In the example, the tables are organised so there is a certain distance between each table, making contact between the children difficult. The tables are thus arranged in such a way that the teacher can see down between the tables, and thus monitor the contact between the rows of tables from the vantage point of the teacher's desk. There is therefore nothing in the classroom's architecture that hinders the teacher's view of the children, and nothing to hinder the children's attention being directed at the teacher. All personal belongings are placed on the shelves on the wall, or left in a small room outside the classroom. Using Latour's own words, one could say that the teacher has delegated part of his/her pedagogical program to the classroom's design and furniture, where particularly the chairs and the two-pupil tables play an important role (the chairs and tables function as what Latour would call a 'non-human, non figurative sign', where the technology more or less demands specific conduct, which does not first need to be interpreted by the users, Latour,

1992, p. 243). As an extra support for the adults' attempts at restricting contact between pupils in class time, an assistant teacher is positioned at the back of the class. The entire classroom's design means that the assistant teacher is made invisible to the children, who, because of the chairs' built-in program, are forced to direct their attention towards the front of the classroom. The assistant teacher has a complete overview of the class and can therefore intervene when the classroom architecture and furniture does not succeed, so that the teacher at the front can continue teaching undisturbed by the pupils' attempts at establishing anti-programs, such as the maintenance of their own social relations.

The above example is taken from a context in which the teacher has interpreted the children's contact with each other as an anti-program to teaching and learning. However, in our fieldwork we also observed examples of how the children's social relations with each other could develop within the pedagogical and architectural program, so that contact between children did not necessarily become an anti-program. The following example is from a grade two class at the 'Early Primary House':

> The children come strolling into the classroom, and a bit later the teacher comes in. The children seat themselves around some round tables and the teacher quietens them down, because they are about to have mathematics. The teacher stands at the board and directs questions at the children at the tables. An assistant teacher sits down at one of the tables, while the teacher explains some exercises on the board, and hands them out to the children. The children sit quietly at their tables and solve the exercises while the teacher and assistant teacher go round and help them. They sit in groups of 4-6 around the tables, and there is no strict regulation of their movements. The tables are so high that the children can stand up and use them, if they wish. Accordingly, a number of the children alternate between standing and sitting at the tables. A couple of them also move around the tables without any protest from the teachers. A boy stands up and sits down and works in a corner where there is a sofa, which is separated from the rest of the classroom by a bookshelf. This is apparently OK with the adults. After being pretty quiet for about 45 minutes, the children begin to move around more between the tables and talk more loudly together. Some of the children are consequently given permission to go out into the hall, if they want a break. However, none go out. One boy joins the boy already sitting on the sofa. They have obviously both finished their exercises, and resort to looking in books and talking together. Another boy shouts across to another table, and the teacher tells him to be quiet and says that he should talk to pupils at his own table instead. (Early Primary House)

In this situation, it is clear that both the spatial organisation and the adult's administration of class time and the classroom, to a greater extent than the last example, allow for contact between the pupils. The tables are not designed to direct the pupils' attention towards the teacher, but rather, because the tables are round, the pupils' attention is directed more towards other pupils at the table or towards a common centre instead. Both the table and the chairs are high and therefore allow the children to stand up and work at the table, and they can easily move between the tables without scraping the chairs when they are pulled out from the table – they can just slide down off the chair, or simply stand up and work. The class is therefore designed so the children can administer their internal relations during class time. They can choose to talk with the other children at the table, they can choose to move over to another table, or they can decide to isolate themselves in the separate sofa corner. The teacher does not have the same amount of overview, as some sit with their backs to the board and can sit in the sofa corner. Neither does the assistant teacher, who in the previous example operated as an extra surveillance tool, operate here as a controller of children's movements and attention, but more as an offer of support when children are working with their exercises.

Even though in this example it is possible for children's contacts amongst themselves not to be construed as an anti-program in relation to the teacher's program and the pedagogical program that is incorporated in and delegated to the classroom's architecture and design, it is apparent that the teacher's program still contains certain behavioural codes for the children. When a pupil attempts to communicate across the tables, for example, he/she breaches the invisible 'sound barrier' the teacher has installed in the classroom.

Externalised and internalised behavioural control

The difference between the pedagogical practice in the two examples is no coincidence but, rather, reflects the two schools' overall pedagogical programs, which are also supported by the schools' architectural built-in program. The first example reflects traditional teacher-centred teaching, where the children's own programs (play, activities, relations, interests) become a disturbance in class as they take the attention away from the curricular content to be learnt. In the second example, the children's own programs are tolerated to a greater extent, and the teacher's control over the children gives scope for activities and interests that can occur alongside children's schoolwork.

If we look at the physical framework, we can say that these two classes represent different levels and types of behavioural control. We can differentiate between two methods of controlling behaviour: an *internalisation* or an *externalisation* of rules. In the first example, the control is largely externalised in that the teacher, the architecture and the layout together ensure that the pupils do not break the rules of conduct, which the teacher wants to apply in the class. In the second example, the physical environment does not exert the same level of control over the children's movements, which to a greater extent suggests that the pupils have internalised the rules of conduct that apply during class time. Using the concepts of internalised and externalised control suggests that control is not removed in the second example (or generally in so-called 'progressive' or 'reform' pedagogy, which it is an example of), but that behavioural control is more removed from the physical organisation and the adult's surveillance of the individual child.

Basil Bernstein discusses this issue when he describes how both pedagogical practice and physical space can be more or less strongly and visibly coded. The visible and strongly coded pedagogy and the visibly coded physical space clearly signal what is allowed and what is expected of the pupils in a pedagogical situation. In the more weakly coded space and pedagogy (reform or progressive pedagogy) it is, however, less clear what is expected of the pupils, and the weakly coded space requires more insider knowledge on the part of pupils in order to be able to know what behaviour is expected within that space.

In a short text on the coding of objects, Bernstein (using bathrooms as an example) describes how rooms may exert more or less control over the persons in the room or delegate more or less control to the persons (Bernstein, 1974, p. 212–215). First, he describes a room, where everything is clean, everything has its own and clearly identifiable place and nothing belonging in other rooms and to other functions may intrude (this is referred to as strong classification), and where all visual and auditory contact with other rooms is sealed off (which is called strong framing). On the one hand, this room is a very visibly controlled room, where any disturbance or deviation from the expected behaviour will be clearly visible (if the soap is not returned to its holder or if a book is left on the floor). Seen from the users' perspective, the advantage of the coding of this room is that the built-in rules of behaviour are easily deciphered and understood: leave everything in its proper place.

The second type of room is an example of weakly coded physical space. Many different kinds of objects have found their way in here, such as books in a basket and postcards on the wall, and the location of each object is not clearly marked, as there is no special container for the soap or for the toilet paper (weak classification). Furthermore the communication with people in other rooms is less tightly controlled, as the door may not have a lock or the lock may be broken (weak framing). At first sight, this room may look like a place where one may do as one wants, but Bernstein's point is that this weakly coded room is not free from rules, but rather the rules of the proper behaviour are left weak or implicit and thus they are harder to decode and more dependent on an adequate prior socialisation. The actual user of this weakly coded room must be able to rely on a built-in program in him or her (prior socialisation) as the program is not clearly communicated by the room itself. In other words, the weakly coded room presupposes a certain type of user; a user who has internalised behavioural control to such an extent that the physical space can 'loosen its grip' on the body and behaviour of that person. Also, the built-in user of weakly coded space in school is a child, who is able to decipher the space; just because physical space is 'loosened up' it does not signal total freedom but rather a freedom under responsibility, a freedom to behave appropriately on one's own accord.

We incorporate Latour's and Bernstein's perspectives in the analysis to remind ourselves that the pedagogy and the physical space described in the second field-note presented above (from the Early Primary House) cannot be understood exclusively in terms of more acceptance of the children's programs at the expense of those of adults. The shift from teacher-oriented teaching, illustrated in the first example, to the greater focus on the child's learning processes, illustrated in the second example, makes instead other demands that the child has to meet. Here, the demands are not so much the outer disciplining of the body (to remain seated with the body directed towards the teacher), but to be able to rely on prior socialisation in order to navigate in a physical and pedagogical space that does not clearly communicate rules of proper conduct and instead communicates a somewhat paradoxical freedom to act responsibly.

The spatial prerequisites of progressive pedagogy

As mentioned above, the differences in the two above-mentioned schools' pedagogical practices reflect the general pedagogical approaches at these schools. However, it is also noticeable that the two schools' different buildings (which are connected to the year they were established) support different types of pedagogical behaviour. Already in the 1970s, Basil Bernstein described how the pupil-oriented so-called progressive pedagogy (which is called the 'invisible pedagogy' in Bernstein's terminology) makes huge demands on school buildings: "the invisible pedagogy presupposes a particular form of primary socialisation *and* a small number of pupils in the class *and* a particular architecture (...) It is an *expensive* pedagogy that stems from an expensive class"[2] (Bernstein, 1974, p. 179). In our own research, we are able to re-visit Bernstein's point that pupil-centred pedagogy is relatively space-demanding, and that a traditionally structured classroom easily becomes a hindrance to new forms of pedagogical practice (Gitz-Johansen, Kampmann & Kirkeby, 2001). A number

---

2 Bernstein connects different codes with the typical modes of socialisation in different social classes. Bernstein argues that the strongly coded pedagogy and spatial arrangements have a similarity with the socialisation in low-education families, whereas the more weakly coded pedagogy and spaces have similarities with the socialisation in more educated families (Bernstein, 2001). Thus, if Bernstein is correct in his argument, we may expect that pedagogies and rooms with weak coding will favour children from certain segments of society whereas what Bernstein calls "underprivileged classes and ethnic groups" will have a harder time behaving adequately in this physical and pedagogical environment. To support his argument of the class base of different pedagogies, Bernstein refers to a study of how the two pedagogies (visible and invisible) historically have been promoted by just the social groups that, according to his theory, would benefit the most from their mode of communication and interaction (Jenkins, 1989).

of the teachers interviewed suggested that the lack of floor space or lack of classrooms appropriate for group work makes it difficult for them to practice anything other than the teacher-centred pedagogy, where pupils sit in rows facing the front. This spatial organisation of pupils partly means that there is space for a lot of children in a relatively small area. Moreover, the allocation of roles means that it is the teacher who should be heard, while the pupils are expected to remain quiet and listen to or answer individual questions, and this makes it easier to separate children. Types of work such as group work and project work obviously do not only require space but also sound isolation between the groups so that they can talk within the group without disturbing the other groups.

Above, we have discussed how different pedagogical programs arrange and utilise physical space in different ways depending on the kind of behavioural control (internalised or externalised) the pedagogical program seeks to exert over the children. It is also suggested that characteristics of the physical space (such as a lack of floor space) may result in teachers exerting more external and visible control than their pedagogical ideals would otherwise have them do.

The children's programs

Above, we have concerned ourselves with two of the groups of actors during the school day: the buildings and other physical artefacts on the one hand, and the pedagogical personnel on the other. Both groups of actors, via their different programs, attempt to structure the school day. A third actor group is the children, who as pupils participate in the school day and bring with them their own intentions and programs. From the above focus on architectural and pedagogical programs, it would be tempting to assume that children live in a so tightly controlled environment that the space remaining for their own intentions and actions is irrelevant. This would fit in with a structural analysis of life in school but as the sociology of childhood has shown, children are actors with their own intentions, interpretations, perspectives and relationships (Corsaro, 1997; James & Prout, 1997; Jenks, Prout & James, 1998; Mayall, 2002). Hence, children's programs (e.g. actions, relationships and intentions) cannot be deduced from the social and physical structures that surround them but must be studied independently although still in relation to the conditions offered by the control exerted and the possibilities offered by adults and physical space.

A characteristic of a large part of the school day is that the children must work hard to fit their own programs (intentions and actions connected to their play, social relations and school work) into the pedagogical and spatial programs through which adults organise the school day. As part of our research into the interaction between children and the school's physicality, we investigated, amongst other things, children's experience of and ways of using the physical space in the three youngest classes in three different school buildings (Gitz-Johansen, Kampmann & Kirkeby, 2001). We investigated, among other things, how the physical space assists and hinders children's attempts to establish their own programs in the school day. Below are some examples of the programs we observed children trying to establish in the school day and which influenced both the physical space and the pedagogical administration of that space:

- The establishment and maintenance of relations with other children throughout the entire school day, to the extent that the spatial organisation and administration of them allowed.
- The use of the room to reshape the school environment to fit their own activities and agendas, although the school environment may be pre-designed by architects and dominated by the adults' expectation that the room after a clean-up returns to 'normal' at the end of the day.
- The use of the room to establish a certain degree of privacy, in order to shield oneself or a small group of children off from the rest of school life.

As mentioned above, the school day is structured by the pedagogical personnel's pedagogical programs, as well as the pedagogical programs incorporated in the school's architecture and design. During the school day, the children's programs are often subordinated by these dominant programs and a part of the building is designed to obstruct the children's own programs, just as teachers also spend a great deal of energy ensuring that the children's programs do not develop or that they develop in harmony with the pedagogical programs. In the event that there is conflict between the children's programs and the pedagogical programs, the children's programs become anti-programs. The children's activities are therefore not anti-programs in themselves but only in the event that they conflict with the school's dominant programs – the pedagogical programs. In the follo-wing, we will elaborate on one of the activities in the school day that children often prioritise but which, depending on the pedagogical context, can often become an anti-program: children's attempts at creating and maintaining rela-tions throughout the school day.

Creating and maintaining relations

Seen from the perspective of adults, children go to school so they can become qualified for later participating in working life and society in general. They are there to learn something. Seen from the children's perspective, learning and becoming qualified are not necessarily the most important part of the school day. From the children's perspective, the creation and maintenance of social relations with other children is an important competitor to the adults' project of

Architecture, pedagogy and children 67

keeping children's attention on the teaching. Depending on the school and the individual teacher's pedagogical profile, the children's attempts at establishing and maintaining social relations may be contested by the teacher's intended use of school time. In the endeavour to keep the attention of children directed towards the teaching, the physical space either assists or hinders. In the first of the two examples from the teaching situations described earlier in connection with the pedagogical programs, the physical space assists in isolating children from each other during class time and facilitates the adults' control of the children's interaction (from Comb School). In the second example (from Early Primary House) the spatial organisation encourages the children to organise themselves in self-chosen groups around tables where their communication can be maintained. Moreover, in this example there is a relaxation of the adults' control over the children's interaction and part of the room is screened off from the view of the adults and therefore reduces their ability to control the children's interaction.

Reshaping physical environment

One instance where the children's programs often become anti-programs in schools and day-care institutions is when children attempt to shape and reshape the physical environment of their everyday life. Kampmann writes in a report about the physical space and children's everyday life in day-care institutions that the physical space's ability to be changed (that things are not bolted down, are not finished and are not pre-defined) is a prerequisite for good play relations between children and for their play to be better (seen from the children's perspective) if it can be altered and reshaped (Kampmann, 1998, p. 24). In contrast to the children's desire to reshape their surroundings, Gulløv and Højlund describe how the physical space in many pedagogical contexts is designed in such a way as to minimise the opportunities for children to leave their marks and traces, and instead supports the adults' intention that the room should be returned to normal before the start of each new day: "There appears to be a lack of understanding of the logic in returning the pedagogical room to normal, that children are only there temporarily, and that their impact on the design and decoration should be superficial and restricted to perishable materials" (Gulløv & Højlund, 2005, p. 33, our translation). What is described here is an adult intention to restrict the opportunities for the children to alter their environment. What is allowed is a limited and controlled decoration of the room with drawings and wall pictures, which on the one hand signal that children's products are valued, and on the other ensure that such products do not disrupt the teachers' and cleaners' daily routines and that the room can quickly be returned to its normal state. This normal state can be understood as neutral and functional (e.g. in relation to cleaning), but it can also be understood as a subordination of children's programs in relation to the other programs (the architect's, the personnel's).

There is a big difference between how children's wish to alter and influence their physical environment is handled in different pedagogical contexts. Among the three schools, which were described earlier, it is particularly in Comb School's teacher-centred pedagogy and control-oriented architecture that the children's alterations and influences are erased on a daily basis by the adults' 'desire for order' (Kirkeby, Gitz-Johansen & Kampmann, 2005, p. 55). In Early Primary House's more pupil-centred pedagogy and less order-oriented architecture, the demand to return the room back to a "neutral" state at the end of the day is lower. Here, children's wooden block constructions are left to take up floor space from day to day, and outside the children built a wooden ship, which, while we were there, was developed into an even bigger ship. These construction projects engaged the children for weeks at a time, and they returned to them day after day.

Finding and creating space for privacy

Schools and day-care institutions are places where the space that each child can inhabit is normally scarce. According to Kampmann, children in most child institutions have much less space than adults find comfortable to remain in for longer periods of time (Kampmann, 1998, p. 36–37). Therefore it is perhaps not surprising that part of children's time in day-care institutions is used to establish some private space in the form of designated territory or, when that possibility is lacking, by directing their attention inwards towards an 'inner space' (Kampmann, 1998, p 14).

The majority of schools and day-care institutions include spaces that are reserved for teachers (the teacher's lounge or the staffroom), where the adults can take a break from all the interactions and relations, which are constantly underway in the areas where children are allowed. However, often little thought is given to children's need for such a possibility for peace, and the opportunity for children to take a break is built into neither the building nor the pedagogical practice. So it becomes part of the children's own programs to establish smaller spaces in the school and day-care institution's everyday life. During interviews, school children told us about how they use the school toilet as a room they can get away to: "If you get upset, you can sit in there. I have also tried it; you can come back out a bit later."

In addition to attempts at establishing a completely private space, children also attempt to create boundaries around their various activities; this often occurs in spite of the physical organisation of the school rather than because of it. It can either be an attempt at creating a space within which to work on their schoolwork, or it can be an attempt at protecting their play relations from being

Architecture, pedagogy and children 69

broken up by other children who move through the space. The following excerpt from our field-notes shows two girls' attempts to utilise the meagre resources available to create some privacy around their interaction and relationship:

> Out on the playground, Mia is standing on the flagstones skipping with another girl. After they have skipped for a short while, they find a corner near the wall, where there is a little outcrop. They take their jackets off and place them tidily in the corner so that they can sit on them. They also take their shoes off and place them nicely beside each other up against the wall, before returning to the flagstones and skipping some more. Not much later they agree that they would rather sit and chat in their corner than skip. They begin to run around the playground collecting milk crates, which they place around their jackets and shoes in the corner. The second girl, who is sitting on the jackets says, "They have to go around me". With their little corner, their jackets and some milk crates, they have made themselves a small designated space where they can sit and chat. They tell each other that they are best friends. The only thing the building gives them is a small outcrop from a wall, which provides them with a frame to build their little intimate sphere out from. Even though a number of older children are playing ball and playing out on the flagstones in front of them, this designated area is apparently enough to give the girls their own private space. (Common Room School)

As this example shows, children can utilise the (however meagre) resources offered by the playground to create some privacy and protection around their interaction.

The goal of this last section has been to understand the ways in which children are not passive objects of architectural and pedagogical programs but, rather, subjects with their own agendas, which they attempt to pursue and fit into the school day.

Conclusion

Above, we have investigated and discussed some ways in which physical space, pedagogical practice and children's own agendas interact in complicated ways to construct everyday life in school. With an empirical point of departure in the three selected schools in the study, we have discussed how pedagogical programs (intention and ideals) are built into the architecture of the school, and thus orchestrate what goes on within these physical frames, but we have also shown how architecture does not determine the way teaching is carried out; teachers must operate within the frames provided by physical space, but teachers must also read and interpret the physical space and to some extent they can manipulate and change their physical surroundings to fit their intentions. Thus, the relation between pedagogical and architectural programs is more or less harmonious or tense depending on how well they match or how much they mismatch.

We have also discussed two ideal-typical pedagogical modalities, which can be termed traditional and progressive pedagogy, respectively, (or in Bernstein's terms: visible and invisible pedagogy) and we have discussed the different ways in which these two pedagogical modalities use space to exert their particular type of social control over the lives and learning of the pupils. In this section we also problematised the existence of a simple relation between pedagogical modality, its use of physical space and children's freedom. Progressive pedagogy and its arrangement and use of physical space may appear to give children more freedom from external control and surveillance of children's bodies, but this may come at the price of more internal control and higher demands on the children's abilities to interpret the codes of conduct inscribed in the school's physical layout and furnishing.

Lastly, we have included children's own programs in the analysis, which has shown how children's actions and intentions are not determined by the practices of adults and the layout of buildings. Children's lives in school are certainly very much structured by the pedagogical and architectural programs, but at the same time children pursue their own agendas, which may fit well into, conflict with or be irrelevant to the pedagogical and architectural programs, which are built into school.

References

Andenæs, A. (1991). Fra undersøkelsesobjekt til medforsker? Livsformsintervju med 4-5 åringer [From Research Object to Co-Researcher? Way-of-Life Interview with 4-5 Year olds]. *Nordisk Psykologi,* no 4, vol.43.
Andersen, P.Ø. & Kampmann, J. (2002). Klasserums- og institutionsforskning [Classroom and Institution Research]. In Andersen & Knoop (eds.), *Børns liv og læreprocesser.* Værløse: Billesø & Baltzer.
Bernstein, B. (2001). Klasseforskelle og pædagogisk praksis [Class Differences and Educational Practice]. In Chouliarki, L. and Bayer, M. (eds.), *Basil Bernstein: Pædagogik, diskurs og magt.* Copenhagen: Akademisk Forlag.
Bernstein, B. (1974). *Basil Bernsteins Kodeteori* [The Code Theory of Basil Bernstein]. Copenhagen: Christian Ejlers' Forlag.
Connolly, P. (1998). *Racism, Gender Identities and Young children.* London: Routledge.
Corsaro , W. A. (1997). The sociology of childhood. Thousand Oaks: Pine Forge Press.
Deegan, J. G. (1996). *Children's Friendships in Culturally Diverse Classrooms.* London: Falmer Press.
Delamont, S. (1976). *Interaction in the Classroom.* London: Methuen.

Delamont, S. (ed.) (1984). *Readings on Interaction in the Classroom*. London: Methuen.
Earthman, G. I & Lemasters, L. (1997). The Impact of School Buildings on Student Achievement and Behavior. A Review of Research. *PEB Exchange*, no 30, Feb.
Freeman, M. & Mathison, S. (2009). *Researching Children's Experiences*. London: Guilford Press.
Gitz-Johansen, T., Kampmann, J. & Kirkeby, I. M. (2001). *Samspil mellem børn og skolens fysiske ramme* [Interaction between Children and the Physical Space in School]. Copenhagen: Rum, Form og Funktion.
Gordon, T., Holland, J. & Lahelma, E. (2001). Ethnographic Research in Educational Settings. In P. Atkinson, et al. (eds.), *Handbook of Ethnography*. London: Sage.
Gulløv, E. & Højlund, S. (2005). Materialitetens Pædagogiske Kraft [The Educational Power of Physical Space]. In Larsen, K. (ed.), *Arkitektur, krop og læring*. Copenhagen: Hans Reitzels Forlag.
Haavind, H. (1987). *Liten og stor* [Small and Big]. Oslo: Universitetsforlaget.
Hammersley, M. & Woods, P. (eds.) (1984). *Life in School: The Sociology of Pupil Culture*. Milton Keynes: Open University Press.
Itoh, Shunsuke (2001). *Children and the Physical Environment in School Settings. Case Studies in Danish Folkeskoler from a Socio-ecological Approach* (www.sbi.dk/arkitektur/undervisningsbyggeri/skolebyggeri/children-and-the-physical-environment-in-school-settings).
Jackson, P. (1968). *Life in classrooms*. New York: Rinehart & Winston.
James, A. & Prout, A. (eds.) (1990). *Constructing and Reconstructing Childhood. Contemporary Issues in the Sociological Study of childhood*. London: Falmer Press.
Jenks, C., Prout, A. & James, A. (1998). *Theorizing Childhood*. Cambridge: Polity Press.
Jenkins, C. M. (1989). *The professional middle class and the social origins of progressivism: a case study of the Ned Education Fellowship* (Ph.D. thesis). London: Institute of Education, University of London.
Jørgensen, P. S. & Kampmann, J. (eds.) (2001). *Børn som informanter* [Children as Informants]. Copenhagen: Børnerådet.
Kampmann, J. (1994). *Barnet og det fysiske rum. Et blik ind i barndommens landskab* [The Child and Physical Space. A View into the Landscape of Childhood]. Copenhagen: Forlaget Børn & Unge.
Kampmann, J. (1998). *Det fysiske rum og børns hverdagsliv i daginstitutionen* [Physical Space and Children's Everyday Lives in Kindergarten]. Roskilde Universitetscenter, Erhvervs- og Voksenuddannelsesgruppen.

Kampmann, J. (2007). Pædagogisk-kritiske og kritisk pædagogiske traditioner [Traditions in Pedagogical Criticism and Critical Pedagogy]. In Andersen, P. Ø., Ellegaard, T. & Muschinsky, L. J. (eds.), *Klassisk og moderne pædagogisk teori*. Copenhagen: Hans Reitzel.

Kinney, L. & Wharton, P. (2008). *An Encounter with Reggio Emilia: Children's early learning made visible*. London: Routledge.

Kirkeby, I. M. (2006). *Skolen finder sted* [School takes Place]. Hørsholm: Statens Byggeforskningsinstitut, Arkitektskolen Aarhus & Kungliga Tekniska Högskolan. Summary (http://www.sbi.dk/arkitektur/undervisningsbyggeri/skolen-finder-sted/)

Kirkeby, I. M., Gitz-Johansen, T. & Kampmann, J. (2005). Samspil mellem fysisk rum og hverdagsliv i skolen [Interaction of Physical Space and Everyday Life in School]. In Larsen, K. (ed.), *Arkitektur, krop og læring*, Copenhagen: Hans Reitzels Forlag.

Kvale, S. (2007). *Doing Interviews*. Los Angeles, Cal.: Sage.

Latour, B. (1999). *Pandoras Hope. Essays on the Reality of Science Studies*. Cambridge, Mass.: Harvard University Press.

Latour, B. (1992). Where are the Missing Masses? The Sociology of a Few Mundane Artefacts. In Bijker, W. E. & Law, J., *Shaping Technology/Building Society – Studies in Sociotechnical Change*, Cambridge/London: The MIT Press.

LeCompte, M. & Preissle, B. (1992). Toward an Ethnology of Students Life in Schools and Classrooms. In LeCompte, Millroy & Preissle (eds.), *The Handbook of Qualitative Research in Education*. London: Academic Press.

Lefebvre, H. (1991). *The Production of Space*. Oxford: Blackwell.

Loisos, G. et al. (Heschong Mahone Group) (1999). *Delighting in Schools. An Investigation into the Relationship Between Delighting and Human Performance*. Pacific Gas and Electric Company.

Mayall, B. (2002). *Towards a Sociology for Childhood. Thinking from children's lives*. Buckingham: Open University Press.

McLaren, P. (1998). *Life in Schools*. Boston: Allyn & Bacon.

Morrow, R.A. & Torres, C.A. (1995). *Social Theory and Education*. Albany: SUNY Press.

Olwig, K. & Gulløv, E. (2003). Towards an Anthropology of Children and Place, in Olwig, K. F. & Gulløv, E. (eds.), *Children's Places. Cross-cultural Perspectives*. London: Routledge.

Paget, Henry (1995). Sociology: After the Linguistic and Multicultural Turns. *Sociological Forum*, Vol. 10, no 4. Special Issue: African Americans and Sociology: A Critical Analysis.

Qvortrup, J., Bardy, M., Sgritta, G. & Wintersberger, H. (eds.) (1994). *Childhood Matters. Social Theory, Practice and Politics.* Aldershot: Avebury.
Rasmussen, K. (ed.) (2006). *Børns steder – steder for børn* [Children's Places – Places for Children]. Værløse: Billesø & Baltzer.
Rorty, R. (1992). *The Linguistic Turn. Essays in Philosophical Method. With two Retrospective Essays.* Chicago: University of Chicago Press.
Skantze, A. (1989). *Vad betyder skolhuset? Skolans fysiska miljö ur elevernas perspektiv studerad i relation till barns och ungdomars utvecklingsuppgifter* [What is the Meaning of the School Building? School's Physical Environment from Students' Perspective Studied in Relation to the Developmental Tasks of Children and Youth]. Stockholm: Department of Education, Stockholm University.
Solomon, Les (1978). Mental Mapping: a Classroom Strategy, *Journal of Geography*, 77:2, Feb.
Thorne, B. (1993). *Gender Play. Girls and Boys in School.* Buckingham: Open University Press.
Walford, G. (ed.) (2008). *How to do Educational Ethnography.* London: The Tufnell Press.
Wargocki, P. & Wyon, D. P. (2008). The performance of schoolwork by children is not affected by short-term electrostatic particle filtration outside the pollen season, in Strøm-Tejsen, P., Olesen, B. W., Wargocki, P., Zukowska, D., Toftum, J. (eds.), *Indoor Air 2008: The 11. International Conference on Indoor Air Quality and Climate.* Copenhagen: Technical University of Denmark.
Weinstein, C. (1979). The Physical Environment of the School: A Review of Research. *Review of Educational Research*, Vol. 49, no 4, Fall.
Woods, P. (1983). *Sociology and the School. An Interactionist Viewpoint.* London: Routledge & Kegan Paul.
Young, M. F. D. (ed.) (1971). *Knowledge and Control: New Directions for the Sociology of Education.* London: Collier-MacMillan.

Interspaces for learning?
A study of corridors in some Swedish schools in a historical perspective

Maj-Lis Hörnqvist

For hundreds of years, teaching and learning have been going on in certain buildings and school is the environment for teaching and learning for all citizens in Sweden. Consequently, school is one of the largest workplaces in modern society, a place that includes adults as well as children and youths. Teaching and learning in school buildings can be understood as the kind of teaching and learning society prescribes as useful and essential for being able to live and work in a proper way as adults. The educational interest in school buildings is old. As early as in the middle of the 19th century, the significance of the building was pointed out by a principal named Siljeström (Sörensen, 1942). In 1856, Siljeström published *Inledning till skol-arkitekturen* (Introduction to School Architecture) and a pamphlet called *Bidrag till skol-arkitekturen* (Contribution to School Architecture) where he emphasizes that the role of the building as educational is a question of vital importance. He asserts that the appearance of the external objects that directly speak to the pupils' senses is just as important as books for their upbringing.

As the world is constantly changing, the school buildings as well as teaching and learning are also constantly changing. From the beginning of the 20th century, pedagogy in school has changed many times, and this influences the perceived need and use of the buildings. As buildings mirror history, and although a built environment is essentially a social and cultural product, it grows older also from a learning perspective.

At the beginning of the 20th century, schools were built for all teaching and learning activities to take place inside classrooms where the teacher was the leading player. Contemporary teaching is more focused on the pupils and their learning and these new preferences makes it interesting to pay attention to school buildings in a new way. Furthermore, if we consider that pupils also bring emotions from spaces outside the classroom into the classroom, these other spaces, which from here on will be called interspaces, must be included in the framework for understanding the educational significance of school buildings. This was confirmed in a previous study of a group of adult students (Hörnqvist, 2000). They explained their wellbeing in school with reference to the shape of the rooms in the building and saw this as a significant factor for their learning. The rooms in school can be understood in a wider perspective than just a place where teaching and learning school subjects is going on. It can also be understood as a place where pupils are influenced and grow by being in a social community in school as well as by learning subjects – a place where they can find out who they are, by just being in school. It can be assumed that the rooms in school play a significant role in this case and these thoughts will be developed later in this chapter.

The purpose of this chapter is to explore the educational significance of some interspaces in school buildings, with special emphasis on corridors. First, the underlying theoretical assumptions about lived space and interspaces are introduced. Design plans and curricula representing each period have been used for a historical contextualisation. Then, the observations and the results of the phenomenological investigation are presented. The results are discussed and interpreted in the light of Otto Friedrich Bollnow's theory of lived space. I conclude the chapter by highlighting the educational significance, related to the theoretical perspective of the lived space and the mutual interplay between people and place.

Lived space and interspaces in the school

One point of departure in this chapter is that we spend time in buildings without reflecting on them, they are taken for granted and as a prerequisite of indoor life. We experience colours, furniture, space, smells, etc. As a consequence, lived places change as people move in and out, daylight changes over the course of the day and so on.

The theoretical perspective is based on Otto Friedrich Bollnow (1963) and his theory of lived space. From a phenomenological perspective, he emphasizes the reciprocity between man and room and that rooms are experienced differently by different people. A room can, for example, be experienced as narrow and limited by one person, while another experiences it as spacious. In other words, the surrounding rooms are dependent on the humans working there and the humans' way of being are dependent on the rooms. Another way of expressing this is to say that the pupils' as well as the teachers' entrance into the school-building means that they *dress* themselves in the room or, in other words, they integrate the room in their way of being (Alerby, 2003; Alerby, Bengtsson, Hörnqvist & Kroksmark, 2002).

Bollnow (1963) presents aspects of the room that I find useful in this study. His division into different aspects of space illuminates how rooms can be interpreted. From his theory about man and space I have chosen *the space of action* (der Handlungsraum), *the mood of the space* (der gestimmte Raum) and *the space of human relations* (der Raum des menschlichen Zuzammenlebens), as central concepts for understanding the interspaces in school.

Interspaces for learning?

Rooms in school

In school we can find different kinds of rooms. There are classrooms and many other kinds of 'rooms' that form a whole – the school. A classroom can be described in a traditional way as the room the class belongs to, distinguished from rooms for special subjects. A classroom in this sense is most common among younger pupils. A broader way of describing a classroom is to include all rooms intended for teaching, including teaching special subjects such as sports centres, rooms for home economics and rooms for handicrafts and woodwork and so on. The latter is a relevant description in this study, to separate the classroom from other kinds of spaces in school, such as corridors, stairs, vestibules and other open places, which can be assumed to be not taken for granted and not reflected upon in teaching and/or learning. Let us call these kinds of spaces in school buildings interspaces (Hörnqvist, 2004). Certainly, there can also be outdoor interspaces of educational interest, for example between different school buildings, but they will not be the subject of discussion in this chapter. In other words, we meet quite a lot of inter*spaces* on our way from the entrance to a certain classroom, all of which are integrated in our way of being. In this chapter interspaces are limited to corridors inside school.

Old school buildings

As long ago as at the beginning of the 13th century, there was in Visby, on the island of Gotland, a school for the bourgeois children in the town. The buildings as well as the content of schoolwork were probably influenced by the church at that time. School was at this time established and supported by private persons, municipalities, rural districts or the church. When the church demanded that even the country people should be able to read, a kind of travelling teaching and learning activity started in people's homes. So, the rooms for teaching and learning were, except in specially designed buildings, situated in people's homes in this period.

A demand for special rooms, adjusted to certain methods of teaching and learning gradually emerged. In the 17th century, the first upper secondary schools were, according to Marklund (1984), permanently established in Sweden, and buildings for this specific purpose were created. Initially, they were large lecture halls, where different teachers taught many pupils at the same time (Landquist & Husén, 1969).

Education was a big issue around 1900 and industrialisation was a challenge in education (Kristensson, 1998). The compulsory elementary schools were established in Sweden in the middle of the 19th century by a law from 1842. At the beginning of the 19th century, teaching was still carried out in very large groups in very big rooms and there was no need for other rooms. Marklund

(1974) describes a situation in school, where there were often about 70 pupils to one teacher, as mechanical drilling without any spirit.

Governmental interest in school buildings was manifested in the first *Normal Design Plans for Elementary Schools* in Sweden in 1865 (Kongl. Öfverintendents-Embetet, 1865). It was a quite detailed description of how to organise, decorate and furnish. Here benches made their appearance with their typical form and we could still see them in schools up to the 1970s, since when they have gradually been replaced by other kinds of tables. There is an extensive chapter in this plan on the classroom; the form and area, how the pupils should be seated, different kinds of equipment, i.e. the teacher's desk, windows, walls and ceiling, heating, ventilation and the significance of neatness and cleanliness. The only room mentioned in the school building besides the classroom was the room for outdoor clothes and lunch packets.

Comments on method

In a study of physical spaces in school, data were collected by means of observations in twenty Swedish schools in order to explore the significance of interspaces in the school building. The selected schools were foremost secondary schools and were strategically chosen to find one school in each city that was typical of the end of 19th/beginning of 20th century, the 1930s, the 1950s, the 1970s and around 21st century in four cities in Sweden (Luleå/Piteå, Stockholm, Jönköping and Gothenburg). All the school buildings selected are still in use, and represent a period of more than a century, 1892 to 2002, in order to visualize the changes in school architecture in Sweden. In this chapter, the main focus is on the interspaces, or more precisely, on corridors in the schools.

The observations of the physical spaces in each school were made during a normal school day and documented with a digital camera. The photos of the corridors were then used to analyze different aspects of the physical interspaces in the schools inspired by a phenomenological approach. Although a considerable variety in the interspaces has been observed within each period, some aspects from each period are prominent and will be the topic of this chapter.

Interspaces in Swedish schools during a century

Greatness at the beginning of the 20th century

The oldest schools in the study are all quite impressive both regarding their size and their interior. They were built between 1892 (Christinaskolan in Piteå) and 1917 (Nordhemsskolan in Gothenburg). They bring to mind palaces and these old school buildings express the importance of school and education at that time.

Interspaces for learning?

To be a pupil educated in a palace-like building probably meant something other than being educated in pavilions that were emerging in the 1960s. This raises the question of what a beautiful environment meant to those people who were there? These school buildings were built after the first *Normal Design Plans* (Kongl. Öfverintendents-Embetet, 1865) had been introduced, and have been rebuilt several times to suit new educational demands. Decoration, furnishing and the importance of tidiness and cleanness were stressed in this plan. Another characteristic of schools from this period is the large front door and the big entrance hall. Whether you are a big boy or a small girl, you would probably feel small in such a big place. There are often broad stairs to the floor above which can emphasize the feeling of smallness. On the other hand, the atmosphere of importance and being someone permitted to learn, and belong to a building that looks like a palace, can be interpreted as meaning that your education is important. Whether the feeling differs depending on whether the school is compulsory or voluntary is debatable. Consequently, at the same time as the pupils can feel like the chosen ones, the size of the building can also mean that they feel diminished.

The size of the building is reflected in the corridors, which were and still are broad, long and with high ceilings.

The long and wide corridors

Schools from this period were originally built for teaching and learning taking place inside the classroom (Kongl. Öfverintendents-Embetet, 1865). Interspaces such as corridors were not mentioned in the first *Normal Design Plans*, but their presence is unmistakable in the old school buildings from this period.

There are long and wide corridors with big windows, originally built for transportation inside the school. In contemporary education, the large areas in the corridors provide the opportunity to create extra working places to satisfy new educational demands. An example of such adjustment is Mariaskolan (see figure 1) where the long corridors have been divided by putting up walls of glass, which give the impression of the corridor being shorter. Mariaskolan was built at a time when schoolwork took place entirely inside the classroom and the corridors were used for walking to and from the classrooms – as a transportation area.

Figure 1: Mariaskolan in Stockholm, built in 1893.

Old corridors equipped for action in contemporary education

This broad corridor in Mariaskolan is equipped for action, with tables and chairs of different heights and in a part of the corridor there are some armchairs, indicating a place for relaxing. The equipment makes the place more homelike. Common to the equipped corridors in this study is the shape of the side corridors, with windows along one side. It seems that daylight plays an important role in choosing places for work or relaxation.

Another kind of corridor found in these old schools today is the central corridor located in the middle of the school, and surrounded by walls without windows on sides. As a consequence, these corridors suffer from lack of daylight and they also lack equipment for work or resting. These kinds of naked places are not places where you stop and rest or do school work. These types of corridors indicate transportation, a passage to lessons.

Interspaces for learning?

Trust and protection or exposition and vulnerability?

There were not many people in these corridors during our visits. It seemed like they were not used for action although they are furnished for this purpose. We can suspect that schoolwork takes place principally inside the classroom and all the classes have breaks at the same time, just as in the old days when the school was built. Does this imply that the teachers gather in the staffroom and have coffee together in the breaks? Without any adult present these, kinds of places could invite harassment and bullying because of their size and lack of people. How frightened could a shy, younger pupil be while passing through a corridor or staircase, on his/her way to the classroom, if, for example there is a gang of older pupils resting there, and if there is no other way to choose? It is difficult to escape from ill-intentioned so called "friends" in corridors and it can be difficult to get help if there are no adults present. But even if there are teachers nearby, they can choose not to care, so the presence of people is no guarantee of not being harassed. The same corridor could, in another situation, be a place for the older pupils to welcome and support younger pupils. People and place mutually influence each other.

Greatness remains in the 30's

The schools from the next period, 1917–1938, are just as impressive regarding size and interior as the schools from the beginning of the 20th century.

In 1920, a new *Normal Design Plans for Elementary Schools* (Kungliga Ecklesiastikdepartementet, 1920) was published which was more comprehensive than the earlier one. It deals with entrances, stairs and cloakrooms, rooms for different kinds of materials, libraries, offices, doctor's consulting-rooms, assembly halls and rooms for a school bath. In addition, there are rooms for special subjects such as drawing, handicrafts and woodwork, cooking, geography and natural sciences. In this plan, the pupils became visible. It pointed out that the school building first and foremost should be a building for the children. The pedagogy of activity was developing in the 1919 curriculum (Kunglig Maj:t, 1919) and the aim was that all the children should feel that being at school was like was being at home. A lot of rooms other than classrooms were also paid attention to, and the influences from John Dewey and the learning-by-doing objectives and pupil-centred teaching and learning activities began to take hold (Isling, 1988).

Corridors for transportation and communication

The corridors found in schools from the beginning of the 20th century were now explicitly mentioned in the new plan from 1920. It suggested that rooms in school could be arranged either according to a corridor system and/or to a system with a hall close to one or two classrooms. In the first case, the corridors could be found along the length of the building, either in the middle of the building, *central corridors*, or on one of the sides, *side corridors*. In side corridor systems, corridors could be found going straight across the building with classrooms on one side and windows on the other. The purpose of these kinds of corridors was accordingly to promote transportation between the different parts in the building, which the plan underlined. In a system with halls, each classroom had its own cloakroom and was most suitable in smaller school buildings (p. 14). This must not be confused with the 'hall school' that emerged in the 1950s. Even if Kristenson (2005) argues that this plan, like the plan before, was intended for schools in small or medium-sized communities, these kinds of side and central corridors were found in school buildings in large towns too, for example in Karl Johansskolan in Gothenburg.

The bareness of central corridors in schools even from the 1930s indicates that they still seem to be used exclusively for transportation between different parts of the school, as originally intended, while some of the side corridors were also equipped for at least resting. The size of the central corridors made it possible to place the now so common lockers there, where pupils could keep their schoolbooks and personal belongings. Also, cupboards for storing different teaching materials in and hooks for outdoor clothes can be found in these side corridors nowadays.

The mood of empty places

Remembering that these schools were built in a period where it was pointed out that school buildings should be buildings for the children, it was underlined that pupils should feel at home in school in the sense that it should offer a friendly and attractive sight to make the building feel like home. Harmonious forms and dimensions as well as subdued colouring were suggested in the *Normal Design Plans* (Kungliga Ecklesiastikdepartementet, 1920). An example of a school built in this period where it is difficult to get that homelike feeling today is Eriksdalsskolan built in 1937–1938 (see figure 2). All the hard and bare surfaces characterizing floors and walls as well as the absence of furniture are striking. Easy to keep clean, but how do the hard surfaces influence those waiting there or passing through to a lesson?

Interspaces for learning?

Figure 2: Eriksdalsskolan in Stockholm, built in 1937–1938.

Take the fluorescent tubes in the ceiling as an example of how small things can reinforce the impression of an institution. Here, it is easy to feel that you are not supposed to stay for a long time. The atmosphere reminds one more of an impersonal waiting room. It is obvious how the equipment of a place can invite certain activities and turn away others. How tempting is it to be in a naked place that reminds one of a corridor in a prison or a hospital in comparison with a more homelike place?

Compulsory school and the need for new space

By about 1940, Swedish society had developed into a technically developed industrial and agricultural society where a growing part of the population wanted a more qualified education for their children (Fredriksson, 1971). However, the 1919 curriculum continued to be applied. In spite of the fact that some new subjects had been added as a result of decisions by the authorities, politicians as well as experts on school considered it to be out of date and incomplete, according to Marklund (1974). Therefore, in 1940 a school commission was appointed and in its instructions we can see the beginning of a new compulsory school emerging, with wider tasks than the former elementary school. The ultimate task of school was broadened to foster pupils in a broader perspective than just to focus on knowledge in subjects. As a result of the growing number of pupils born in the middle of the 1940s along with broadened and prolonged education, the shortage of school buildings became obvious in the 1950s (Marklund, 1971). In 1959, the government approved a program for school buildings that resulted in considerably increased subsidies for temporary school buildings. During the years that followed, a large number of pavilions were built.

In 1946, the school commission, composed by experts, was replaced by a political commission, which established the 9-year compulsory school, the first six of which were attended by all pupils (Marklund, 1974). The commission underlined the most important role of school as supporting personality development and providing education to function as democratic citizens. To reach that goal, school had to change its working methods from questions and answers to more activating and individualizing methods. The commission proposed an inclusive differentiation of pupils, i.e. individualized teaching in the class (Marklund, 1971). This change influenced the building of schools.

New rooms needed

Marklund (1974) points out that it was now suggested that the traditional way of organising schoolwork, teaching in class, should be replaced. Group work and individualized work were introduced as complements and an alternation between class, group and individual work was recommended. Group work was seen as benefiting cooperation between pupils as well as individualization, and the library was mentioned as a suitable place for such work. Because of the new working methods, the need for additional workplaces appeared. Up to now, the classroom had been the main workplace in school. In the 1950s, there was a breakthrough for specially designed rooms in school, and rooms for different subjects replaced the classrooms and were recommended in secondary school and in upper secondary school. The need for transportation spaces was accentuated because the pupils had to walk from one room to another inside the school many times a day. During this period, the centrally situated cloakrooms emerged.

Open places emerge

In the 1950s, central corridors and side corridors remained and hall systems were developed. Open places made their entry. Hall systems were a modification of corridor systems where central corridors were developed into halls, which extended through the building and had balcony-type galleries that facilitated the traffic through the building. The hall could be used as an assembly

Interspaces for learning?

hall for the pupils in school as well as a place for breaks when the weather was bad.

One example of an open place shaped in form of the hall system mentioned in 1920 in the *Normal Design Plans* (Kungl. Ecklesiastikdepartementet, 1920) is Sturebyskolan, built in 1951 (see figure 3).

Figure 3: Sturebyskolan in Stockholm, built in 1951.

Tables and sofas are placed at one end of the balcony surrounding the hall. In spite of the fact that our visit took place during a normal school day, very few pupils could be seen in the public places in the school.

If there are no people in these kinds of places, it could mean that most of the work is still going on behind closed classroom doors with no need to use other spaces for teaching and learning.

Schools built between 1940 and 1965 in general have corridors with one wall of windows and side corridors. They are often not as wide as those at the beginning of the 20th century. Even in a quite narrow side corridor in Norra Örnässkolan in Luleå, there were tables and chairs near the window, as extra workplaces for pupils. Here the corridor is divided by a screen, which minimizes the risk of visual disturbance (figure 4).

Figure 4: Norra Örnässkolan in Luleå, built in 1952.

Depending on what kind of work pupils are doing, this place could facilitate learning, being close enough for the teacher to check the work or for pupils to call for help from the teacher. Sitting here outside the classroom doing schoolwork in peace and quiet while the rest of the class is talking out loud seems like a good learning environment. It could also be a suitable place if most of the class is working on something in silence, and some of the pupils need to talk about their work.

Factory of education in the 1970s

Even if the political commission from 1946 implied a change in working methods, *one teacher – one class* was stipulated in the curriculum before the 1962 curriculum (Skolöverstyrelsen, 1962), and the classroom was still central in teaching and learning. This curriculum prescribed teaching and teachers of special subjects, and co-operation between subjects in thematic work was recommended to make schoolwork meaningful to pupils. The common basic education covering a broad section of working life was central. Social up-

Interspaces for learning?

bringing was still highlighted as important and group work was presented as a way of promoting cooperation and a feeling of fellowship in schoolwork. The importance of the pupils feeling at home in school, which was first mentioned in 1920, was still emphasized in the 1962curriculum.

In the 1970s the design plan prescribed by National Council of Educational Administration remained in force, and continued to be the norm while constructing school buildings. The design plan contained norms for different kinds of rooms, not the entire school building. Schools with rooms for special purposes, for example, computer rooms and teachers' workrooms, were built, but classrooms were still the most important rooms in school.

In the 1970s, the compulsory school was extended by adding three new forms and schools grew bigger. A new curriculum was introduced which emphasized pupils' individual choices. The schools built at this time were often situated in the centre of a suburb, close to a church and a shopping centre. Like the curriculum from 1962, the new curriculum from 1969 (Skolöverstyrelsen, 1969) suggested class, group or individual work as organisational forms for learning activities. A combination of these forms was recommended, which meant special demands on the rooms. In conjunction with an investigation about the inner work of school (SIA), the idea of "a home classroom" or home divisions was presented (Johansson, 2000).

Open spaces as 'public' places

The ideology of an open school (Pluckrose, 1975) influenced the big open study areas, a kind of interspace developed in the late 1960s and early 1970s. The idea behind the open plan schools was to give flexibility in teaching, activities and timetabling, which resulted in the fact that the freest and most unprogrammed space – the corridor – was considered as a waste in the most orthodox applications and tended to disappear in its old shape (Markus, 1993, p 94). They were, however, still visible in a modified shape in our contemporary schools at the end of the 20th and the beginning of the 21st century.

Many of the open spaces from the 1970s were built in the form of study halls, surrounded by classrooms, which blocked the daylight and made them quite dark. In school buildings from the 1970s, the lockers have moved from corridors to big halls (see figure 5). In the breaks, all the pupils can be in these halls at the same time to change their school books to be ready for another subject. The area can thus be quite crowded with pupils during these perhaps 15 minutes and then be empty again.

Figure 5: Skälltorpsskolan in Gothenburg, built 1972.

This could probably be a stressful situation with the pupils to jostling each other while trying to quickly change books for the next lesson. A situation like this could most likely occupy the pupils' thoughts and contribute to the mood for learning afterwards.

Locker halls, study halls and quite narrow corridors as passages to different parts of the school are typical interspaces that emerged in schools from the 1970s.

The feeling of home, that was underlined by curricula from 1920 to 1969 has now faded away and is difficult to experience in these factory-like buildings. However, the homelike environment is perhaps more related to the furnishing and decoration inside the school building than the building and rooms as such. But these kinds of school buildings can be thought of as offering minimal options to create a homelike feeling. It is difficult to feel at home in these big, dark halls. The daylight that was stressed in earlier design plans does not seem to matter anymore. This can be explained by the development and use of artificial light that has been more common.

Interspaces for learning?

Home areas in contemporary schools

The contemporary school buildings tend to differ more in shape than school buildings from earlier periods. They are not restricted by any norms from the Government and are often planned with their starting point in some educational vision of how to work in the particular school. Cooperative work between architects and educators precedes the building itself. This means that school buildings can look very different depending on the unique situation of the specific region. But the contemporary educational trends can be identified in schools irrespective of geographical area, such as open spaces and light colours.

The curriculum from 1980 (Skolöverstyrelsen, 1980), underlined teachers' teamwork and teaching units, which implies large changes in the ways of working in school compared with the curriculum from 1969. In a study by Krupinska (1987), it is stated that 95% of the existing schools were built before the curriculum from 1980 was implemented, and there is some uncertainty on the part of the Government as to whether this should be regarded as an obstacle or not. Nevertheless, The National Board of Education in Sweden as well as some of the authorities were convinced of the increased need for school buildings due to the new curriculum. In the study by Krupinska, the most obvious problem with the school buildings reported by a majority of the 203 municipalities and rural districts in the study was the insufficient adjustment to the curriculum.

From 1994, cooperation between school, pre-school and before-and-after school activities was stressed in the curriculum that was introduced in 1994 (Utbildningsdepartementet, 1998). The rooms in school have to be suitable for activities for caring for the pupil throughout the day. A shift from big classes in big places to schools with home areas has taken place.

A variety of interspaces emerge

One expression of the 'home areas' is that the classrooms often have their own entrance from the outside. The educational influences from the 1970s can be seen in the shape of the small group rooms connected to each classroom. Different kinds of open areas can be seen and a mix of short corridors and open areas are common in contemporary schools. In Trädgårdstadsskolan, built in 2002, the pupils worked near their classroom where there were open working areas, which, together with the classrooms, formed their "home area" (see figure 6).

Figure 6: Trädgårdsstadsskolan in Stockholm, built in 2002.

Safety

The furniture in the open working place could be assumed to contribute to a homelike environment. If pupils feel safe in this environment it could be when they are surrounded by classmates and teachers nearby; however, people close by is no guarantee of safety. In contemporary schools, the long corridors have become shorter and pupils can reach their "home area" from outside or via stairs in the middle of the school.

Another way of shaping transportation areas is in the form of an angle, like the corridors in Kråkbergsskolan. The bend in the corridor gives an impression of it not being that long. Even in a narrow place under a staircase, pupils were found working, similar to Örnässkolan from the 1950s. Sitting there, you cannot avoid the fact that people are passing by, which can be disruptive. Choosing this kind of workplace must mean that there is some benefit in being there, for example, learning or socialization.

Interspaces for learning? 91

Some examples of the open, public places that appeared at the end of the 1990s can also be found in Kråkbergsskolan, built in 1992 (see figure 7), Ale Gymnasium built in 1995 and in Trädgårdsstadsskolan built in 2002.

Figure 7: Kråkbergsskolan in Luleå, built in 1992.

This place is used both as a café and as a workplace, and is situated in the middle of the school, like a hub. Pupils as well as teachers could be seen there all the time during our visit, indicating a well-used area. It is equipped with tables and chairs and park benches. In one corner there is a loom and some old furniture, trying to make it more homelike. The openness means that teachers as well as pupils can be there at anytime. The chance of anything unpleasant happening there is reduced by the openness of the place, provided that the people who are there care about what happens.

Aspects of lived space

Bollnow (1963) points out some different aspects of the room, where I have used *der Handlungsraum* (space of action), *der gestimmte Raum* (mood of the space) and *der Raum des menschlichen Zuzammenlebens* (space for human relations) as concepts to understand the interspaces in the school. These three aspects of space will here be discussed in relation to their educational significance.

Space of action

Bollnow describes the space of actions as the space in its entirety, where tools for the working humans' everyday use are situated. These tools do not stand by themselves. They have to be considered as a part of the whole and their expression and significance depends on the context.

School buildings mirror the working methods that were predominant at the time when they were built. The shape of the school building bears the stamp of official directions from that time. Although a building is perhaps more than one hundred years old, attempts to make the rooms more suited to modern teaching and learning can be seen. We can see a trend from arranging places for schoolwork in corridors in school buildings from the beginning of the 20th century to specially designed spaces near the classrooms in contemporary school buildings. These newly built areas serve as spaces for schoolwork as well as spaces for doing things together in a more social way.

The equipment in places, including their spatial arrangement, indicates what actions are going on there. The long naked corridors from the beginning of the 20th century invite the pupils walking along them, while the same kind of corridor from the same period, but equipped with chairs, tables and sofas seems to invite other kinds of actions, for example, sitting down doing schoolwork, talking or just resting. These differences of arrangement can be understood as differences in teachers' and principals' pedagogical ideas.

Since the room influences humans and humans influence the room, it is obvious that the pedagogy used in a particular school influences the way the physical spaces are used and perceived and vice versa. One belief is that old school buildings facilitate a traditional way of working to a higher degree than supporting new working methods. There are, however, examples of old schools that have been adapted; for example, using corridors for schoolwork, which illustrates the fact that the people working in the building have influenced their environment. A small narrow space does not mean that it is useless as a workplace. If the working methods in school require spaces for small groups, unexpected places may be perceived as potential workplaces and become adequately equipped as, for example, under a staircase. Teachers accordingly have the power to extend or restrict the use of rooms in school.

So, in the same way that buildings mirror history as stated at the beginning of this chapter, a building also mirrors the current educational ideas and working methods used. What actions take place are shaped by the type of equipment. Space for walking through, waiting or working is based on the physical conditions of the corridor and the arrangement of objects that makes certain actions more or less possible (Bollnow, 1963).

What does it, then, mean to sit and work in these kinds of public places that these corridors are? It obviously means that there is a risk of being disturbed by friends passing by. It can also be enjoyable with some friendly small talk as a welcome break in one's work. Teenagers spend a lot of time trying to figure out who they really are, and learning about oneself takes place everywhere, inside the school building as well as outside.

Mood of the space

Every place has a particular mood that pushes its way into and captures our senses, according to Bollnow (1963). Some examples of this are churches and schools. But the reciprocity of the human and space implies that a certain place can be experienced differently by different people, but also differently by the same person on different days, or even times of the day. Things in the place, the weather outside, light, colours, sounds and smells are such things that influence the mood of a certain place as well as the mood of the person entering the place.

Regarding the significance of belonging, trust and protection, as Bollnow (1989; 1994) puts it, something has obviously happened in the last century. The ideal of a homelike environment that arose in the plans at the beginning of the 20th century has differed in form in schools from different periods. In the old schools, we can see attempts to make side corridors more homelike, while in contemporary schools the building of separate entrances to each class area can be understood as serving the same purpose. Consequently, the homelike environment mentioned in old curricula and design plans does not seem to depend on the physical frames. Much has been done in old school buildings to convey that kind of feeling, for example, walls painted in light colours, sofas and tables placed near big windows as in Mariaskolan in Stockholm, built in 1893, while there are examples of newer buildings from the 1970s lacking that kind of home feeling. Hard surfaces with florescent tubes can create a feeling of a waiting room and the dark and big study halls from the 1970s remind one of the atmosphere in factories. But a cold and bare place is not cold and bare by its nature. It is influenced by the people working there and at the same time influences the people. This means that the same place can be understood differrently depending on whether it is empty or inhabited by students and/or teachers.

Space of human relations

In social life at school, space has to be shared. It can be shared in fellowship, but when this fellowship is lost, the fight for living space emerges and fighting and bullying can appear (Bollnow, 1963).

Open areas that are available to everybody in school, can mean places to meet other pupils, fall in love, get angry, curious, frightened and so on. In the old schools, corridors were the most un-programmed places, as Markus (1993) also states, and this is still the case. While the classroom was in the power of the teacher, corridors were places where pupils could meet on their own terms. Everything could happen here, good as well as bad situations could develop, and some of them could improve learning while others could be experienced as obstacles. Today, we have, besides the corridors, other kinds of open, public places that serve this purpose in school.

The development of bigger areas can facilitate human relations. The presence of many people in the same place makes it possible to sit together in friendship and get acquainted with new friends. At the same time, there is a risk of fights and meeting enemies. Public places in school, such as corridors and other open areas can for example be perceived as threatening, especially if you are a shy, lonely pupil having to enter these places to get to or from your destination. Examples of places for human relations are the common open spaces in contemporary schools where people gather over a cup of tea or a newspaper, while others are sitting there working. Another example from older schools is the large wide corridors where many pupils could gather waiting for the classroom door to be opened by the teacher.

The place can accordingly be a place for caring and loving, or it can be a place for envy and competition. There can also be a fight between space to share and space for oneself. Bollnow (1963) states that when the real cooperation and life together start, then the fight for living space is overcome because in real cooperation, both parties are winners and neither is a loser.

Concluding Remarks

The room of action, the room of human relations and the mood of the room are different aspects used to understand the significance of interspaces, such as corridors, in the school.

Depending on the people present, the impression of places varies. A building as such cannot be responsible for things that can happen, even if it offers possibilities or restrictions. What matters is what people do with these possibilities and restrictions. With the interplay between people and places, interspaces can provide opportunities and limitations in relation to the values of the people being there and the physical space can challenge the creativity of the teachers, pupils and principals to create interspaces needed to promote good teaching and learning according to the working methods chosen. They can also be experienced as an obstacle. Nevertheless, they affect teachers and pupils working there, their feeling of belonging and wellbeing, safety and security, and consequently they affect the mood for learning and learning itself, whatever the learning object is. Experiencing feelings, good or bad, can in different ways contribute to the mood of pupils beginning lessons and accordingly they can influence learning of subjects as well as learning about oneself. In times when there are economic restrictions, where society cannot afford new school buildings, the opportunities of existing school buildings have to be utilised in a pedagogical perspective.

So the conclusion is that we should not ignore the interspaces and their significance in supporting or restricting actions, human relations and moods of educational significance. Teachers and principals have the power to create these places to promote students' learning and wellbeing in school.

Acknowledgements

This chapter is part of a research project called "The Significance of the Physical Building in Teaching and Learning", supported by The Swedish Research Council. The paper is based on a symposium organised by Jan Bengtsson at the annual conference of the Nordic Educational Research Association in Reykjavik in 2004 with contributions by Eva Alerby, Jan Bengtsson, Patrick Bjurström and myself. I am truly indebted to this research group for critical comments on my paper.

All photos in the chapter were taken by the author.

References

Alerby, E. (2003). *Learning as Embodied Experience*, Paper presented at the conference of the Nordic Educational Research Asscociation, Copenhagen, Denmark, 6–9 March 2003.
Alerby, E., Bengtsson, J., Hörnqvist, M.-L., & Kroksmark, T. (2002) *Reflections on the Signification of the Architectonic Formation in School from a Lifeworld Approach.* Paper presented at the European Conference on Educational Research, Lisbon, 17–20 September 2002.
Bengtsson, J. (2003). *Formation of Space in the Classroom.* Paper presented at the The European Conference on Educational Research in Hamburg, 17–20 September 2003.
Berg, F. (1942). *Hur folkskolestadgan tillkom* [How the Elementary School was Created]. Stockholm: Svensk läraretidnings förlag.

Bollnow, O. F. (1963). *Mensch und Raum* [Man and Space]. (8th edition 1997) Stuttgart: Kohlhammer.
Bollnow, O. F. (1989). The Pedagogical Atmosphere. *Phenomenology + Pedagogy,* 7, 5–76.
Bollnow, O. F. (1994). Vara-i-rum och ha-rum [Be-in-room and Have-room]. *Nordisk Arkitekturforskning,* 7, 111–119.
Eriksen, A. (1996). *Skolen som ett laerested og et vaerested* [The School as a Place for Learning and Being]. Olso: Dafolo.
Fredriksson, V. (1971). De parallella barndomsskolorna [The Parallell Childhood Schools]. In V. Fredriksson (ed.), *Svenska folkskolans historia, sjätte delen – skolutvecklingen 1942–1962* [The History of the Swedish Elementary School]. Stockholm: Stiftelsen för förvaltning av Sveriges allmänna folkskollärarförenings tillgångar.
Hörnqvist, M.-L. (2000). *Erfarenheter från "Kunskapslyftet" – våren 2000* [Experiences from the "Raising Knowledge". Spring 2000]. Luleå: Luleå University of Technology. Unpublished manuscript.
Hörnqvist, M.-L. (2004). *Physical Interspaces in Teaching and Learning.* Paper presented at Nordic Educational Research Association's 32nd Congress, Reykjavik, Iceland, March 11–14 2004.
Isling, Å. (1988). *Kampen för och emot en demokratisk skola. Det pedagogiska arvet.* [The Struggle For and Against a Democratic School. The Pedagogic Inheritance] Uddevalla: Sober.
Johansson, S.-Å. (2000*).* Med avsikt att förbättra, förbilliga eller fördyra. Om skolbyggnadeer, deras finansiering och hyressättning under 1800- och 1900-talen [With the Intention to Improve, Make Cheaper or Make More Expensive. About School Buildings, its Financing and Rent Setting During the 19th and 20th Centuries]. In S. G. Nordström (ed.), *Utbildningshistoria 2000.* Uppsala: Föreningen svensk undervisningshistoria, 9–54.
Kongl. Öfverintendents-Embetet (1865). *Normalritningar till folkskolebyggnader jemte beskrivning.* [Normal Design Plans for Elementary Schools]. Stockholm.
Kristensson, H. (1998). Skolhuset inför ett nytt sekel. [The School Building at a New Century]. In S-Å Nilsson & L. Vinge (eds.), *Kring 1900*, Nyhamnsläge: Gyllenstiernska Krapperupstiftelsen.
Kristenson, H. (2005). *Skolhuset. Idé och form.* [The School Building. Idea and form]. Lund: Signum.
Krupinska, J. (1987). *Hur är det med skolhusen?* [What is the Situation About the School Buildings?] Stockholm: Skolöverstyrelsen.
Kungliga Ecklesiastikdepartementet (1920). *Normalritningar till skolanläggningar för folkskolan jämte anvisningar och beskrivningar.* [Normal Design Plans for Elementary School Buildings]. Stockholm.

Kunglig Maj:t (1919). *Undervisningsplan för rikets folkskolor* [Teaching Plan for the National Elementary School]. Stockholm: P. A. Norstedt och söners förlag.
Landquist, J., & Husén, T. (1969). *Pedagogikens historia*. [The History of Pedagogy]. Lund: Gleerups.
Markus, T. A. (1993). *Buildings and power*. London: Routledge.
Marklund, S. (1971). Skolplanering och skolbyggnader [Planning Schools and School Buildings]. In V. Fredriksson (ed.), *Svenska folkskolans historia, Vol. 6*. Stockholm: Stiftelsen för förvaltning av Sveriges allmänna folkskollärarförenings tillgångar, 221–240.
Marklund, S. (1974). *Vår skola* [Our School].Stockholm: Bonniers.
Marklund, S. (1984). *Skolan förr och nu. 50 år av utveckling* [The School in Former Times and Now. 50 Years of Development].Stockholm: Liber.
Pluckrose, H. (1975). *Open school, open society*. London: Evans Bros.
Skolöverstyrelsen (1944). *Folkskolebyggnader. Anvisningar och bestämmelser angående byggnader för folkskoleväsendet.* [Elementary School Buildings: Directions and Regulations Concerning Buildings for the Educational System]. Stockholm: Kungl. Skolöverstyrelsen.
Skolöverstyrelsen (1962). Läroplan för grundskolan, Lgr 62 [Curriculum for the Compulsory School, Lgr 62]. Stockholm: Kungl. Skolöverstyrelsen.
Skolöverstyrelsen (1969). *Läroplan för grundskolan,Lgr 69* [Curriculum for the Compulsory School, Lgr 69]. Stockholm: Liber.
Skolöverstyrelsen (1980). *Läroplan för grundskolan,Lgr 80* [Curriculum for the Compulsory School, Lgr 80]. Stockholm: Liber.
Sörensen, A. (1942). Skollokaler och skolinredning [The Rooms and Equipment in School]. In V. Fredrikssson (ed.), *Svenska folkskolans historia, tredje delen – det svenska folkundervisningsväsendet 1860–1900* [The History of the Swedish School – the Swedish Elementary Educational System 1860– 1900]. Stockholm: Bonniers.
Utbildningsdepartementet (1998). *Läroplan för det obligatoriska skolväsendet, förskoleklassen och fritidshemmet. Anpassad till att också omfatta förskoleklassen och fritidshemmet, Lpo 94.* [Curriculum for the Compulsory School, Lpo 94]. Stockholm: Utbildningsdepartementet.

The school building as experience

Hansjörg Hohr

The physical environment in general and the school environment in particular are of fundamental importance to education. For instance, the school building makes you walk, climb and descend stairs, and it defines a relatively narrow range of body postures and movements while excluding others. There are also air quality and temperature, typical odours, noises and visual impacts. The physical environment leaves its sensuous impressions in such a direct and straightforward way that it seems to bypass higher mental mediation or to make it irrelevant or secondary. Nonetheless, the interaction of the body with the school environment far transcends the purely physiological. Thus, the demands on the school environment are complex, and in the following I will try to identify central criteria.

On methodology

There is little research on school buildings in the science of education due to the fact that the topic is pertinent to architecture. Another reason may be the traditional neglect of the human body in education. If there is a possible contribution by a theory of education on the topic it has to come from the realm of social sciences and the humanities. There are several options. Environmental psychology has long investigated natural and artificial surroundings and their impact on individuals. Its main approach is to identify and analyze preferences for certain environments. There is a strong tendency to conceive of these preferences as natural or even native. For example, there is a suggestion that people, due to processes in natural history, prefer plants in their living spaces since their ancestors have spent thousands of years in the woods (Cold, 2001). There are more specific studies on aesthetic preferences, which can give us ideas about what kind of environments the users of school buildings prefer and enjoy (Cold et al., 1998; Nasar, 2000; Seland, 2001).

The alternative to the environmental psychological approach is the sociological approach. Basil Bernstein (1977), for example, could show that the concept of space is based on pragmatic codes that reflect the control and power relations within a given society, and that the school building is a reflection of a certain pedagogical way of thinking. He points to two fundamental patterns, namely classification and framing. Classification refers to the strength of the boundaries between contents. In terms of education, this means how strictly various subject matters are confined or integrated with each other. In terms of school buildings, it means how specialized or multifunctional space is, how closed or open the school environment is. Framing refers to the structure "of the context in which knowledge is transmitted and received" (Bernstein, 1977, p. 88), to the way in which the learning activities are moulded, to the degree of integration or segregation of social groups with respect to age, sex, abilities, interests, roles (like teacher and pupil), school and home are in a given school education. The implication of framing for space is as obvious as that of classification. A weak framing allows for a wide variety of learning activities and requires open and multifunctional spaces while strong framing requires closed spaces which enable a high degree of central control by a teacher over pupils.

A similar approach to the school building is that of *space syntax research*, founded by Bill Hillier and Julienne Hanson (1984; Hillier, 1996; Hanson, 1998) (see also Berg, 1987; Bjurström, 2004; Koch, 2004; Markus, 1993). Not unlike Bernstein, Hillier conceives of a spatial system as a "virtual social system", i.e. a symbolic reflection of the structure of social relationships. Consequently, Hillier and Hanson call space a "morphic language" with its specific *space syntax*.

The above-mentioned approaches can cast light on important aspects of the school building, but their scope is rather narrow. However, this is not the place for detailed criticism and I want to just point out that the lack of concepts regarding the cultural aspect is conspicuous and problematic.

Interaction and Subjectivity

The frame of understanding that I am going to propose is inspired by Alfred Lorenzer's (1981) and John Dewey's work (1925, 1934, 1938). Doing research in the tradition of the Frankfurt school, Lorenzer studied the relationship between the individual and society and especially how contradiction and oppression in the structure of society is reflected on the level of psychological structure. After language theory studies (Lorenzer, 1970 a, b) in *Destruction of language and its reconstruction* and *Critique of the psychoanalytic concept of symbol*, he turned to what he called a "materialistic theory of socialization" (Lorenzer, 1972, 1974). In his last work in 1981, he turns to the criticism of the Second Council in Rome, which resulted in the rejection of catholic liturgy with devastating effects on the space system of catholic churches.

There are three criteria Lorenzer wants to satisfy in his approach. First, socialization theory must see the human being as a being with drive, which is the irrefutable insight of Sigmund Freud and of psychoanalysis. The organism is thus not limitlessly mouldable but has with it demands from its own natural history. Second, the theory must show the human being as societal, i.e. take into account Marx' insight that the human being is an "ensemble" of societal conditions. Thus, the structure of society has to be taken into account, not as the

The school building as experience

sum of individual or inter-subjective actions but as a factor in its own right. Third, the theory must be able to show the human being as a subject, able to be spontaneous and take deliberate action and to generate or create herself or himself. This is the legacy of the humanist tradition and has been argued in depth by, for instance, Immanuel Kant.

Lorenzer looks for a synthesis of these factors in the pragmatist tradition, more precisely in the concept of interaction by George Herbert Mead. In Lorenzer's view, biology and society are dialectically mediated in the interaction between the individual and its world, and the individual as subject takes form within the evolving interaction. In the interaction between the infant and its caretaker, for instance, in the form of holding the child and feeding it, a biological demand meets with cultural patterns of child-rearing, and these are dialectically synthesized in the "agreement situation" resulting in the concrete interaction between child and caretaker. Thus, from the very beginning, biology and culture are present as elements in the ongoing interaction, although not in an additive manner, but inextricably synthesized on the level of interaction. Seen from this perspective, interaction is neither determined by biological demand nor cast in a certain cultural pattern, but both contribute substantially to it.

As disturbances in caretaking show there are, though, clear limits to the range of possible agreements between biological demand and cultural offer. The child's cry could be interpreted as a sign of such a disturbance. The prime-ordeal interaction, we may call it the sensuous or pre-symbolic interaction, is reflected on the psychological level in the first and fundamental psychological structure. Whether there is subjectivity from the outset of the individual's life is a matter of debate. With respect to the child, Lorenzer reserves the designation subjectivity for the symbolically mediated interaction, thus first when the child enters the world of symbolical meaning is it able to discriminate between self and object and establish self-consciousness[4]. Only then is it meaningful to conceive of the child as a subject. This does not mean that there is a the lack of subjectivity in pre-symbolic interaction. Here, subjectivity must be attributed to the interaction itself[5]. A comparable position is taken by Daniel N. Stern (1985, 1998), while Colwyn Trevarthen (1998) and his school and Stein Bråten (1998) find grounds to talk of a "primary inter-subjectivity" already in the incipient interaction between child and caretaker.

---

1   This position seems to be based on Mead's distinction between gesture and significant symbol. While the exchange of gestures proceeds on the basis of stimulus and reaction, the conversation of significant symbols uses signs that carry a shared meaning.
2   From the standpoint of the adult, the interaction is symbolically mediated. This fact does not, however, make the interaction symbolic from the standpoint of the child. For the pre-symbolic child, there is just the circular pattern of action and reaction. There is certain self-awareness but not the clear distinction between self and world as we know it from symbolic interaction.

Inspired by Lorenzer's distinction of different levels of interaction, I propose to analyze the individuals' interaction with the school building on three levels of experience, of feeling, of aesthetic experience and of conceiving. These levels are defined by the varying role of emotion and the varying mode of cognition involved. To some extent, this distinction allows for the integration of research findings drawn from different methodologies.

To feel the world

There are a multitude of approaches to the question of how the infant relates to the world on a pre-symbolic level. Inspired by the philosopher Susanne Langer (1942), I propose to call the pre-symbolic experience *feeling*. In this sense, "feeling" designates the *experience of feeling the world in sensuous interaction* with it. The question of pre-symbolic experience is not only relevant to the child's development but to experience in general. When we enter the world of symbolic meaning, we do not stop feeling, even though some aspects of experience become more distinct, conscious and open to communication and reflection. In part, perhaps for the most part, experience remains on this level.

Dewey (1934) has pointed out that experience is constituted in the unity of action, emotion, cognition and communication. As to cognition, Jean Piaget (1952) with the concept of sensorimotor intelligence has given a differentiated account of what the pre-symbolic child is capable of. Thus feeling is cognitive as it constitutes the basic cognitive structure of the individual. Psychoanalysis, on the other hand, taking disruptive and seemingly uncontrollable behaviour as a point of departure, was led to the discovery of destruction of experience and thus forced to concentrate on the role of emotion and social interaction in experience. In any case, feeling is not as predominantly cognitive as Piaget's theory suggests, and psychoanalysis has made a strong claim to the pivotal role of emotion in experience. Moreover research by Trevarthen (1998) and his group showed that pre-symbolic experience, feeling, is highly communicative and that the pre-symbolic child almost from the outset discriminates between social interaction with its reciprocity and interaction with inanimate objects. They even observed a musical quality to the proto-symbolic conversations between infant and caretakers (Trehub, 1990; Trehub et al., 1993). In this context, one should also mention the seminal work of Maurice Merleau-Ponty (2002) who pointed out that the experience of the world is based on the body and that there is no experience without it.

When studying the effect of architecture on the organism, there is, thus, the layer of pre-symbolic experience to consider which emerges from the darkness of sheer bodily appreciation. Many of the findings of environmental psychology, I think, relate to this level of experience. Kaplan (1987, 1992) has

The school building as experience

given an interesting contribution even though its theoretical underpinning in the form of evolutionary theory is problematic.

	understanding	exploration
immediate	coherence	complexity
inferred, predicted	legibility	mystery

Figure 1: Kaplan's "Framework of Predictors of Preference".

He proposes two main criteria, one is the mode of mediation where he distinguishes between the immediate and the anticipated; the other criterion is the mode of cognition where he distinguishes between understanding and exploration. At the level of immediacy, the organism requires a certain degree of coherence in the surroundings, of unity of perception and of transparency. However, the organism also requires a challenge of complexity, a certain degree of excitement by the mystery. On the level of mediation, the organism needs predictability and understanding which, however, is contrasted and counterbalanced by the need for a certain degree of novelty and opportunity to explore.

Kaplan's categories seem to exclude the pre-symbolic experience since, for example, "understanding" should be impossible before the child enters the world of concepts. However, Kaplan develops his categories on the basis of evolution. They represent the elementary cognitive discriminations that are established on the pre-symbolic level and thus belong to feeling. The same is valid for Nazar's and Purcell's model (1992) who propose a balance between familiarity and interest in the surroundings. When the Hungarian biologists I. and M. Hargittai (1994) propose symmetry as a "unifying concept" they, indeed, refer to the complex balance of contrasting qualities that make themselves felt long before a symbolic mode of experience.

Even though these basic qualities of the environment are experienced on a pre-symbolic level, the qualities themselves may have a cultural origin. Just to give an example of a school practice in Norwegian schools: there is a widespread rule that at the end of the day, chairs in the classroom should not be left standing on the floor but put on the desks, making the room ready for the subsequent cleaning by the cleaning personnel. As a consequence, unoccupied chairs are often allowed to remain standing on the desks throughout the school day. Thus, it is a frequent experience to see a pupil sitting at a desk with a chair standing close to his/her elbow. It makes one wonder what visual patterns of this kind communicate to the pupils in the classroom with respect to "coherence" and "complexity", "legibility" and "mystery".

Even though one can understand why these culturally based qualities may be prominent in the feeling (see p. 4) of the school environment, there are other factors with a direct, physiological impact such as air quality and temperature, light, cleanliness, and – as a whole – the rhythm of the building which Dewey (1934) has pointed to as the dynamic principle in the flow of action and counter-action in the process of differentiation and integration in experience.

In some respects, the observation that teachers and pupils are bodies in need of a physiologically unstressful but stimulating environment may seem trivial. Having and being a body is the most obvious trait of being human. Still, this is an aspect that tends to get drowned by functional considerations of a disembodied education. It should, though, be the first and last thought in the planning of a school building.

Aesthetic experience of the world

The school environment does not only communicate on the level of feeling but also at a level of experience, which is mediated by sensuous symbolism. I call it *aesthetic experience*[6]. It represents perhaps the most complex mode of experience.

First, a few words on aesthetic experience as a concept. It seems clear that when the child enters the world of symbols, and the experience becomes symbolically mediated there is fundamental change in its outlook on the world. Theorists from disparate traditions and disciplines have seen symbolic play as the decisive step or, rather, as the medium of this step into the symbolic world. The German poet and philosopher Friedrich Schiller observed 200 years ago:

> From this play of freely associated ideas, which is still of a wholly material kind, and to be explained by purely natural laws, the imagination, in its attempt at a free form, finally makes the leap to aesthetic play. A leap it must be called, since a completely new power now goes into action; for here, for the first time, mind takes a hand as a lawgiver in the operation of blind instinct, subjects the arbitrary activity of the imagination to its own immutable and eternal activity, introduces its own autonomy into the transient, and its own infinity into the life of sense (Schiller, 1967, p. 209).

Although, informed by pragmatism and Dewey, we do not subscribe to Schiller's juxtaposition of instinct and mind, the qualitative change in experience has been commented upon by many scholars. The moment the child starts to play, activity is not longer a reaction to stimuli but action based on thought.

---

3 The term refers to a mode of experience, which, in the Scandinavian languages, is called "oplevelse" (Danish), "opplevelse" (Norwegian), "upplevelse" (Swedish) and in German "Erleben".

Symbolic play is the source of the multitude of aesthetic activities and opens the door to a new world. It gives rise to a specific kind of experience.

I will call the interaction that gives rise to aesthetic experience *aesthetic activity*. The symbolism mediating it I will call *sensuous symbolism* or form. Thus, the school building is not only a physical object but also a sensuous symbol that communicates on many levels.

Aesthetic activity is understood here as a synthesis of the (pre-symbolic) feeling and the systems of sensuous symbolism, forms that are offered by culture. In the concrete aesthetic activity these moments are synthesized, sensuous-symbolic meaning is *appropriated*. Form, then, is not an expression of feeling, since feeling is manifested in pre-symbolic interaction only, but the medium by which feeling is transformed into aesthetic experience. Also, form is not a casting mould that renders aesthetic experience into a certain shape. However, the synthesis between feeling and form is never complete as there will always be aspects of feeling remaining outside awareness. If total synthesis were possible, there would be total knowledge. But even though the synthesis necessarily must be incomplete, one must distinguish a successful synthesis from an unsuccessful, good form from bad form. The good form liberates feeling and corresponds to a certain degree to Dewey's "an experience". In the good form there is the experience of fulfilment and elation because an un-articulate, pre-symbolic experience has been freed and delivered into an adequate form and has thus been transformed into conscious experience. The bad form on the other hand warps and adulterates feeling. This quality makes form one of the most powerful media of propaganda and manipulation. Bad form, thus, may result in a crippling sensuous-symbolic interaction. An advertisement for cigarettes, for example, may capture our need for mastery, adventure and freedom and confound them thoroughly. The Nazi architecture may turn our will to live into a death wish (Lorenzer, 1981) and the wish for revolt against oppression and abuse by those in power into unconditional submission and "identification with the aggressor" (Lorenzer, 1981).

The synthesis of feeling and form may also fail for other reasons. A certain form system or tradition may be unknown and therefore inaccessible. Fears and harm from the past may prevent us from being receptive to a certain form. I have tried to sort out the various layers of aesthetic experience on the basis of the analysis of a fairy tale (Hohr, 1993).

In aesthetic experience one becomes aware of oneself as a conscious relationship with the world. Thus, knowledge in aesthetic experience is not clear-cut, objective or subjective, but relational, subject-in-world knowledge. Once this level of experience is established, interaction can be reflected upon.

By comparing the artistic with scientific experience, Ernst Cassirer (1944) has pointed out some distinct features of artistic experience, which, to a certain extent, may be valid for aesthetic activity in general. While science aims at a simplification of the world by breaking it down into distinct objects, by classifying them, by making concepts and by identifying patterns and rules that govern the relationships between the objects, artistic experience aims at complexity, wholeness and emotional intensity of experience. While there is clear self-consciousness in aesthetic experience there is not the emotionally detached eye, which is the hallmark of conceiving. Instead, balancing closeness and distance, aesthetic experience echoes the original immersion into the world, giving rise to an emotionally intensive experience.

Where would one start in the analysis of school environment and school building as sensuous symbolism? Perhaps one should, like David Canter (2001), start with symbolic universals of place, which he identifies as *identification, specification* and *enclosure*[7]. This means that a school environment should be formed in a way that identifies the kind of activities meant to take place, specifies these activities and defines them in space. If this is true, then the school environment is nothing less than a symbolic presentation of what a school is. It presents ideas about what kind of socialization is supposed to take place, whether it is supposed to be an introduction into community life or a place of knowledge, whether knowledge is thought of as individual acquisition or as cultural appropriation (Schubert, 2009), whether knowledge is a matter of listening, reading and writing or a matter of bodily experience in conjoint activities (Dewey, 1916). Clearly, the school building is permeated by cultural and social rules, and there is little or no chance of there being an educationally neutral environment. Thus, starting with Canter's (2001) idea about the *identity* of place, one is confronted by a fundamental educational question and grounds for perennial strife.

However, sensuous symbolism is multifaceted, including ritual, myth, play, festivity, art, social intercourse. Each of these facets may have their own legitimate demand and may, thus, be able to contribute to a good school environment. Why, then, not start with everyday life aesthetics, let us say at the level of the modest flower arrangement on the dining table. Transferring this criterion to the school environment, one has to ask whether the pupils are met with a welcoming and friendly smile by the environment or whether it speaks of neglect and indifference. Clearly, there is much the pupils and teachers themselves can do in order to improve the appeal by upholding standards of order, cleanliness and ornamentation. But friendliness is definitely a valid criterion for the more lasting elements of the environment as well, and its value and importance to learning activities can hardly be overestimated.

---

4   These symbolic universals have, of course, nothing to do with archetypes in the Jungian sense, but seem tied to the basic means of orientation of the body in the world. To this extent, they are close to Piaget's thought on the child's construction of the Euclidian space.

The school building as experience

One could think of everyday life aesthetics as the pivot of aesthetic activity, which is surrounded by a manifold of aesthetic modes that are of importance for the school environment. One of these, and very much akin to friendliness, is that of play or, rather, the playful. Unfortunately, there is a tradition of conceiving of play as an opponent and competitor to work. Here is not the place to argue that this is not so and is even a harmful misunderstanding. However, many scholars have made a successful case of play being an integrated part of every experience especially in the exploring phases, some even declaring the playful to be the validity criterion of experience (Dewey, 1934). In any case, the clear-cut segregation of play and work in the traditional school environment is based on an erroneous assumption and should be corrected as soon as possible.

In his analysis of the aesthetic, Hans-Georg Gadamer (1986) has underlined the importance of festival and celebration as the medium of establishing and confirming the experience of community and of belonging. Thus they are of utmost importance since they emphasize the kind of activities that constitute school and celebrate their value. Even though these occasions are rare breaks in school life, the school environment should have spaces that are adaptable to these festivities.

A further aspect of the aesthetic is the fine arts, which should be reflected in the school environment in a twofold way. The most obvious is that there must be spaces that are adaptable for artistic work such as music, painting, etc. The other is that the school environment as such is designed as a work of art and captures the purpose of the school in a meaningful way. Even though the artistic aspect is not the sole aspect as there are many others, it is a value in its one right. It comprises also less stable components such as various objects of art, paintings, sculptures, installations and the like.

Ethos of school buildings

There is, however, one aspect of the aesthetic that deserves special attention, namely what I call the religious or the moral aspect. Here, *religious* is not understood with respect to the belief in the supranatural or God, but as the moral foundation of human existence, with respect to the fundamental values one *believes* in and is *committed* to. It is what gives life its purpose and meaning, like justice, love, friendship, or money and power as the case may be. I would suggest that the moral foundation on which we build our lives is constituted by aesthetic experience and mediated by form. In contrast, concepts are vital tools in dealings with the world. But they are not able to offer emotional and moral meaning to life. The production of meaning takes place at the level of aesthetic experience, of aesthetic activity. The point here is not that one could or should do away with discursive forms of moral reasoning of the kind, for instance, Habermas (1990) or Kohlberg (1984) advocate. *Moral* aesthetic experience is not an alternative to moral *discourse* but its prerequisite. Moral discourse may help us reach the right decision; moral aesthetic experience, however, makes us moral beings. Thus, moral education begins with aesthetic experience, with moral communication and reasoning in aesthetic experience. School buildings, then, are significant structures as they speak to the users about what is and what should be going on and thus reflect a certain *ethos,* which poses the question of what kind of ethos one should demand from a school environment.

Although this is not the place for a thorough ethical investigation, I will suggest some elements in order to give an idea of the scope of the question. The core demand is that the school building should express a *desire for life.* This is certainly a quality that is desirable in every architectural form. But it is essential in a school, in a place of growth and learning, as there is simply no more important and fundamental educational purpose. What else should pupils learn but to love life itself? Thus, the school building should meet the pupils with a warm, welcoming and encouraging smile, it should comfort them when they meet adversity, and it should inspire and applaud their efforts. It should, in sum, enhance their self-esteem and celebrate their existence.

The desire for life has, moreover, an intrinsic relationship to what one could call the more narrow ethics of school, i.e. the ethics of learning, of investigation and of committed work. It is difficult to imagine a desire for life without a lively curiosity about its various aspects. Thus, besides a desire for life a school building also should express a *desire of investigation.* It should meet the pupil with a friendly invitation and encouragement to get down to work and to find out about life and the world. The various media of investigation should be given a prominent, accessible and not intimidating place in the environment.

The aesthetic experience of *community,* of being part of a common enterprise, of social belonging is also intrinsically related to the desire for life and desire for investigation. Being with others is not only one of the delights of life but a necessary prerequisite of life. Emotional isolation, on the other hand, is not only torment and illness but inconsistent with life. Moreover, investigation and construction of knowledge is social, communicative and relational in its nature. Learning is a cooperative enterprise. Thus, a school building should express, invite and encourage a *sense of* and *desire for community,* for togetherness and reciprocity. It has to reflect a social unity, formal and informal communication. This demand includes, of course, the opportunity for privacy as well since community is incompatible with social coercion.

One last element of the ethos of the school building should be mentioned, namely the sense of freedom. There may not be a desire for life without it. Schiller (1976) pointed to the realm of play as the place of human freedom and bliss. Playfulness may not only make for a pleasant and supportive environment. It may also be directly related to favourable learning conditions. One could argue that the absence of various constraints, of moral, emotional and instru-

The school building as experience

mental coercion in play allows for an exploration of perception and concepts, of emotions and moral demands, of individuality and community (Hohr, 2002, 2006).

I conclude this short excursion into the ethos of the school building with the idea of religiosity in the sense of the later work of Dewey (Retter, 2005). There is a religious aspect to education in the sense that education is or should be based on the belief in the possibility of growth of the individual, of the community and of humanity. The moral and religious basis of education should be reflected in the school building. Architecture that scorns its users, that speaks of neglect, carelessness and utter indifference, is destructive indeed.

Conceiving of the world

In discussing the evolution of the linguistic system and digital communication, Bateson (2000) comments:

> I do not think that any animal without hands would be stupid enough to arrive at so outlandish a mode of communication. To use a syntax and category system appropriate for the discussion of things that can be handled, while really discussing the patterns and contingencies of relationship, is fantastic (2000, p. 371).

Bateson argues for a systemic connection between discursive symbolism, linguistic system and instrumental action. I concur in that with the emergence of discourse and concepts there appears a third kind of experience that constitutes the world of things. In discourse, the relational experience of aesthetic experience is complemented, perhaps to a certain degree substituted and synthesized into an objectifying experience. By conceiving the world, we take a step back in order to single out objects for our attention and for our emotionally detached scrutiny. The relationship between aesthetic experience and *conceiving* is, though, not yet well understood. Bateson (2000) has pointed out that while animals exclusively communicate on an analogical level, they do not come even close to the diversity and complexity of human expression. This fact indicates an interdependence of these two forms of experience. How they are related to each other is, however, beyond the scope of this article.

Concepts are constructed in what I call discursive symbolic interaction. In this kind of interaction, aesthetic experience and offers of conceptual meaning are synthesized into concepts and the conceptual experience. Since discourse, as Cassirer pointed out, aims at a simplification of experience, large parts of aesthetic experience will remain outside this synthesis. Another way of putting this is by saying that art expresses what cannot be stated – not at all, not yet or not anymore. As in the case of form, here, one must also distinguish between a good and a bad synthesis. Lorenzer (1970 a, b) has studied this problem in depth under the title of destruction of language.

What matters in the context of school buildings is that one must consider the level of discursive symbolic interaction and accord it a careful examination. A school building communicates on the level of concepts and labels, even though this level is marginal compared with the others. There may be, though, a fluid transition from the sensuous-symbolic to the discursive-symbolic. The design of the entrance, for instance, indicates through its design on the level of aesthetic experience whether the users are welcome or just a nuisance, but it indicates also on the level of conceiving, perhaps in writing, that here is the main entrance, or whether this is entrance B or C, or entrance North or South. In any case, it is nice when a building tells the users where they may find certain places or persons. This is especially important for e.g. the parents who do not visit the school regularly. One may also use some letters in order to indicate that the building is a school and the name of the school.

Once inside the building, there too should be discursive help available as regards where to find a specific room or type of person. Of course, one can always ask for directions, but a generous supply of pointers signals consideration for and care of the users. Again, the parents are in this respect an easily overlooked party although indispensable as an ally for the school.

The functional meaning and aspect of architecture

School buildings also have an instrumental function that is understood by means of concepts and discourse. I think Bateson is right, that conceiving and discourse are specialized tools for handling things, for communication and reflection on the instrumental aspect of action. The same is suggested in Dewey's concepts *secondary experience* and *statement*. In any case, education and instruction require functional spaces and equipment. The space structure must allow pupils and teachers to coordinate and cooperate, to read and write, to be by themselves and to join each other in activity, to have access to a diversity of sources of information. There must be easy access to recreation spaces and rooms for special activities involving books, data, media, music, arts and gymnastics. There must be places for preparation, cooperation, instruction and counselling for the teachers, to mention just a few of the functional requirements.

However, what is appropriate and functional depends on understanding what a school is and reflects, even ambiguities in this respect. Bernstein's code theory is not a diagnostic apparatus that shows which code is operating in a certain institution. Rather, it helps us to understand school as the place of conflicting functions, interests and concepts of education. Bernstein's code theory allows for a distinction between the individualised appropriation of knowledge in accordance with the collection code operating with strong classification and

The school building as experience

framing and a personalized appropriation in accordance with the integration code, which operates with weak classification and framing. The latter is more or less the basis of educational progressivism and reform.

The organization of space differs substantially whether we conceive of schooling in the sense of collection code or of integration code. The strength of classification, for instance, is reflected and communicated quite clearly in the degree of geographic integration of the various rooms in a school building. A long corridor feeding a series of classrooms may express a strong classification, while a cluster of rooms with landscape solutions may indicate a weak classification. Likewise, a classroom with rows of tables facing the blackboard would suggest a strong framing while clusters of tables facing each other and with easy access to the school library, to computers and to the Internet may indicate weak framing.

Under the rule of collection code, there is a clear-cut social hierarchy, well-defined borders of subject matter and of progression, early and rigorous selection, sparse horizontal cooperation between pupils, between teachers and between school and parents. Under the rule of integration code, the appropriation of knowledge is seen as a joint enterprise and effort. The ethos of the school building sketched above would be consistent with the integration code. There would be close cooperation between school and parents, between teachers, between pupils. The principle of organization of knowledge would be inspired by everyday life and the problems that are meaningful and within the grasp of the pupils. There would be an emphasis on the autonomy and self-regulation of learning processes and of the pupils.

Concluding remarks

There are at least three levels on which one should consider the school building. There is the level of pre-symbolic interaction and feeling, which defines the range and scope of experience. This level is about the fundamental needs and requirements of the body. The school building takes part in the formation of feeling, but its quality is also decisive for the quality of synthesis. One might not like it, but it is time to realize that pupils and teachers are and have bodies.

The next level is the level of sensuous-symbolic interaction, aesthetic activity, which is mediated by form. This level plays a fundamental role in the development of morality and identity. The school building is a powerful communicator of the ethos of education, both because of the level of communication, sensuous-symbolic, and because of its ubiquitous character, its relentless action and its inescapability. If it does not express and support a good ethos, a constructive, meaningful education may not be possible. In addition, the spatial structure presents ideas about what kind of education and instruction are supposed to take place.

There is, then, the level of discursive-symbolic interaction. Not only does this level support and facilitate the orientation of the individual, it is also important for coordinated action and various levels.

There is, last but not least, the aspect of functionality of the school building. This is perhaps the most obvious, traditionally the most considered, although not the easiest to master, since there are competing and, as Bernstein suggests, inconsistent models and ideas of instruction. The challenge for architecture lies in reconciling the requirements and the communication of the various levels and aspects. Each must be considered in its own right. But they also need to be aligned and brought into agreement with each other.

References

Bateson, G. (2000). *Steps to an Ecology of Mind.* Chicago: University of Chicago Press.
Berg (de Jong), M. (1987). *Spatial aspects of social organization – a study of buildings for daycare.* Göteborg: Chalmers tekniska högskola.
Bernstein, B. (1977). *Class, Codes and Control. Vol. 3.* (2nd ed.) London: Routledge.
Bjurström, P. (2004). *Att förstå skolbyggnader* [Understanding School Buildings]. Diss. Stockholm: Kungliga tekniska högskolan.
Bråten, S. (1998). Intersubjective Communion and Understanding: Development and Perturbation. In S. Bråten (ed.), *Intersubjective Communication and Emotion in Early Ontogeny.* Cambridge University Press, 372–382.
Canter, D. (2001). Health and Beauty: Enclosure and Structure. In B. Cold (ed.) *Aesthetics, Well-being and Health. Essays within Architecture and environmental aesthetics.* Farnham: Ashgate Publishing, 49–66.
Cassirer, E. (1944). *An Essay on Man: an Introduction to a Philosophy of Human Culture.* New Haven, Conn.: Yale University Press.
Cold, B., Kolstad, A., & Larssæther, S. (1998). *Aesthetics, Well-being and Health – Abstracts on Theoretical and Empirical Research within Environmental Aesthetics.* Oslo: Norsk Form.
Cold, B. (2001). Beauty. In B. Cold (ed.), *Aesthetics, Well-being and Health. Essays within Architecture and Environmental Aesthetics.* (1st ed.). Ashgate Publishing, 67–92.
Dewey, J. (1916). *Democracy and Education.* In J.A. Boydstone (ed.) (1980): The Middle Works, 1916, Vol. 9. Carbondale and Edwardsville: Southern Illinois University Press.
Dewey, J. (1925). *Experience and Nature.* In J.A. Boydstone (ed.) (1981): Later Works, 1935–53, Vol. 1. Carbondale and Edwardsville: Southern Illinois University Press.

Dewey, J. (1934). *Art as Experience*. In J.A. Boydstone (ed.) (1987): Later Works, 1935–53, Vol. 10. Carbondale and Edwardsville: Southern Illinois University Press.
Dewey, J. (1938). *Experience and Education*. In J.A. Boydstone (ed.) (1988): Later Works, 1938-39, Vol. 13. Carbondale and Edwardsville: Southern Illinois University Press.
Gadamer, H.-G. (1986). *The Relevance of the Beautiful and Other Essays*. Cambridge: Cambridge University Press.
Habermas, J. (1990). *Moral Consciousness and Communicative Action*. Cambridge: Polity Press.
Hanson, J. (1998). *Decoding Homes and Houses*. Cambridge, U. K.: Cambridge University Press,
Hargittai, I. & M. (1994). *Symmetry: A Unifying Concept*. Bolinas, California: Shelter Publications.
Hillier, B. & Hanson, J. (1984). *The social logic of space*. Cambridge, U. K.: Cambridge University Press.
Hillier, B. (1996). *Space is the Machine*. Cambridge, U. K.: Cambridge University Press.
Hohr, H. (1993). Det normative i folkeeventyret – mellom mytisk regel, moralsk prinsipp og spilleregel [The Normative in Fairy Tale – Between Mythic Rule, Moral Principle and Game Rule]. *Nordisk Pedagogik*, 3, 158–172.
Hohr, H. (2002). Illusion – How Friedrich Schiller can Cast Light on *Bildung*. *Journal of Philosophy of Education*, 3, 487–501.
Hohr, H. (2006). *Friedrich Schiller über Erziehung: Der schöne Schein* [Friedrich Schiller on Education: The Beautiful Semblance]. Bad Heilbrunn: Klinkhardt.
Kaplan, S. (1987). Aesthetics, Affect and Cognition: Environmental Preference from an Evolutionary Perspective. *Environment and Behavior*. 19, 3–32.
Kaplan, S. (1992). Environmental Preference in a Knowledge Seeking Knowledge Using Organism. In J. H. Barkow, L. Cosmides, and J. Tooby (eds.) *The Adaptive Mind*. New York: Oxford University Press, 535–552.
Koch, D. (2004). *Spatial Systems as Producers of Meaning: the Idea of Knowledge in Three Public Libraries*. Stockholm: KTH – School of Architecture.
Kohlberg, L. (1984). *The Psychology of Moral Development: the Nature and Validity of Moral Stages*. San Francisco: Harper & Row.
Langer, S. K. (1942). *Philosophy in a New Key. A Study in the Symbolism of Reason, Rite, and Art*. Cambridge, Mass.: Harvard University Press.
Lorenzer, A. (1970 a). *Kritik des psychoanalytischen Symbolbegriffs* [Critique of the Psychoanalytic Concept of Symbol]. Frankfurt am Main: Suhrkamp.
Lorenzer, A. (1970 b). *Sprachzerstörung und Rekonstruktion. Vorarbeiten zu einer Metatheorie der Psychoanalyse* [Destruction of Language and Re-

construction. Preparations to a Meta-Theory of Psychoanalysis]. Frankfurt am Main: Suhrkamp.
Lorenzer, A. (1972). *Zur Begründung einer materialistischen Sozialisationstheorie* [On the Rationale of a Materialistic Theory of Socialization]. Frankfurt am Main: Suhrkamp.
Lorenzer, A. (1974). *Die Wahrheit der psychoanalytischen Erkenntnis. Ein historisch materialistischer Entwurf* [The Truth of Psychoanalytic Understanding. A Historical Materialistic Outline]. Frankfurt am Main: Suhrkamp.
Lorenzer, A. (1981). *Das Konzil der Buchhalter. Die Zerstörung der Sinnlichkeit* [The Council of the Bookkeepers. The Destruction of Sensuousness]. Frankfurt am Main: Europäische Verlagsanstalt.
Markus, T. (1993). *Buildings and Power. Freedom and Control in the Origin of Modern Building Types.* London and New York: Routledge.
Merleau-Ponty, M. (2002). *Phenomenology of Perception.* London: Routledge.
Nasar, J. L. (2000). The Evaluative Image of Places. In W. B. Walsh, K. H. Craik, & R. H. Price (eds.), *Person-Environment Psychology: New Directions and Perspectives* (2nd ed.). Mahwah, N. J.: Lawerence Erlbaum Associates Publishers, 117–168.
Piaget, L. (1952). *The Origins of Intelligence in Children.* New York: International University Press.
Purcell, A. T. and Nasar, J. L. (1992). Experiencing Other People's Houses. *Journal of Environmental Psychology 12*, 199–211.
Retter, H. (2005). Education and Democracy as Spiritual Experience. Liberal and Anti-Liberal Aspects of John Dewey's Criticism of Religion. *Panorama.* Vol. 17, 1–15.
Schiller, F. (1967). *On the Aesthetic Education of Man in a Series of Letters.* Ed. and transl. by E. M. Wilkinson & L. Willoughby. Oxford: Clarendon Press.
Schubert, W. H. (2009). *Love, Justice, and Education. John Dewey and the Utopians.* Charlotte, N. C.: Information Age Publishing.
Seland, G. (2001). *Voksne og barns inntrykk av skolens estetiske utforming.* [Adults' and Children's Appreciation of the Aesthetic Design of the School]. MA thesis at the Institute of Psychology, NTNU – Norwegian University of Science and Technology, Trondheim.
Stern, D. N. (1985). *The Interpersonal World of the Infant.* New York: Basic Books.
Stern, D. N. (1998). The Interpersonal World of the Infant: a View from Psychoanalysis and Developmental Psychology. London: Karnac.
Trehub, S. E. (1990). The Perception of Musical Patterns by Human Infants: the Provision of Similar Patterns by their Parents. In M. A. Berkley and W. C.

Stebbins (ed.), *Comparative Perception, Vol. 1.* New York: Wiley, 429–59.

Trehub, S. E., Trainor, L. I., and Unylc, A, M. (1993). Music and Speech Processing in the First Year of Life. *Advances in Child Development and Behaviour*, 2, 1–35.

Trevarthen, C. (1998). The Concept and Foundations of Infant Intersubjectivity. In S. Bråten (ed.), *Intersubjective Communication and Emotion in Early Ontogeny.* Cambridge University Press, 15–46.

About the authors

Jan Bengtsson is a professor at the Department of Pedagogical, Curricular and Professional Studies, University of Gothenburg, Sweden. He has developed a life-world phenomenological research approach for educational and human studies. He was the founder of the Nordic Society for Philosophy of Education and its president for the first ten years. He is visiting professor at the University of Agder in Norway and has also been visiting professor at the University of Helsinki, Finland, and the University of Oslo, Norway. His current research is focused on the practice of pedagogical professions. His book publications include *Sammanflätningar: Husserls och Merleau-Pontys fenomenologi* [Intertwinings: Husserl's and Merleau-Ponty's phenomenology] (several editions), *Den fenomenologiska rörelsen i Sverige* [The phenomenological movement in Sweden] (1991), *Allmänmetodik, allmändidaktik* [General methodology, general didactics], co-authored with Tomas Kroksmark (1993), *Fenomenologiska utflykter* [Phenomenological excursions] (1998), *Med livsvärlden som grund* [With the life-world as point of departure] (several editions), *Utmaningar i filosofisk pedagogik* [Challenges in philosophy of education] (2004), *Å forske i sykdoms- og pleieerfaringer* [Researching experiences of illness and care] (2006), *Fenomenologi och arkitektur* [Phenomenology and architecture], special issue of *Nordisk Arkitekturforskning* (7/1, 1994), co-edited with Finn Werne.

Patrick Bjurström was trained as an architect at the Royal Institute of Technology in Stockholm, Sweden. Between 1970–1999 he was employed/co-owner of ORIGO/Höjer & Ljungqvist Architects. In 2004, he was awarded a PhD at the Royal Institute of Technology in Stockholm with the thesis *Att förstå skolbyggnader* [Understanding school buildings]. He is currently employed by Stockholm City Planning Office.

Thomas Gitz-Johansen is associate professor at the Department of Psychology and Educational Research, Roskilde University in Denmark. In the last decade he has researched and published in areas such as the social and political formation of childhood, children's interaction with physical space, educational policy and education in culturally diverse schools and kindergartens. He has published *Samspil mellem børn og skolens fysiske rammer* [Interplay between children and the physical frames of the school], co-authored with Jan Kampmann and Inge Mette Kirkeby (2001), and *Den multikulturelle skole – integration og sortering* [The multicultural school – integration and sorting] (2004).

Hansjörg Hohr is Professor of Education at the Norwegian University of Science and Technology (NTNU) in Trondheim, Norway. He studied education, psychology and philosophy at the University of Innsbruck (Austria) and Oslo (Norway) and worked for 11 years in teacher education in Tromsø and Trondheim. The main area of his research is philosophy of education and aesthetics. His most recent book is entitled *Gesellschaft, Religion und Ästhetik in der Erziehungsphilosophie John Deweys* [Society, religion and aesthetics in John Dewey's philosophy of education] (2009).

Maj-Lis Hörnqvist is Associate Professor of Education at Umeå University and Luleå University of Technology (leave of absence), both in Sweden. She was director of a practice-based research school at Luleå University of Technology. Her main research interest is contextual prerequisites of teaching and learning in school. She received a PhD in 1999 with the thesis *Upplevd kompetens – en fenomenologisk studie av ungdomars upplevelser av sin egen kompetens i skolarbetet* [Experienced competence – a phenomenological study of young people's experiences of their own competence in schoolwork].

Jan Kampmann is a professor and research director at the Department of Psychology and Educational Research, Roskilde University in Denmark. For several years he has been involved in ethnographic and policy-based research related to the institutionalised everyday life of children and young people, their learning processes, resistance and strategies in positioning themselves in these everyday settings, focusing on the impact of social background, gender and ethnicity. He has published *Samspil mellem børn og skolens fysiske rammer* [Interplay between children and the physical frames of the school], co-authored with Thomas Gitz-Johansen and Inge Mette Kirkeby (2001).

Inge Mette Kirkeby is a senior researcher at the Danish Building Research Institute, Aalborg Univeristy in Denmark. She is an architect with a PhD in building conservation from Aarhus School of Architecture, Denmark, and a Dr Tech in school buildings from the Royal Institute of Technology in Stockholm, Sweden. Her main research interests are the interaction between education and architecture and the exchange of knowledge between research and practice. She has published *Samspil mellem børn og skolens fysiske rammer* [Interplay between children and the physical frames of the school], co-authored with Thomas Gitz-Johansen and Jan Kampmann (2001), and *Skolen finder sted* [The school takes place] (2006).

www.ingramcontent.com/pod-product-compliance
Ingram Content Group UK Ltd.
Pitfield, Milton Keynes, MK11 3LW, UK
UKHW021839140426
5217IPUK00022B/1515